Phobiapedia

Conceived, edited, and designed by
Marshall Editions
The Old Brewery
6 Blundell Street
London N7 9BH, UK

ISBN 978-0-545-34929-1

Publisher: James Ashton-Tyler
Creative Director: Linda Cole
Editorial Director: Sorrel Wood
Design: Ali Scrivens
Editorial Project Manager: Emily Collins
Project Editor: Elise See Tai
Production: Nikki Ingram
Picture Research: Claire Newman

Originated in Hong Kong by Modern Age
Printed and bound in Dongguan, China, by Toppan Leefung

10 9 8 7 6 5 4 3 2 1   11 12 13 14 15

First edition, September 2011

For the fearless and fantastic Isaac and Finn, Arielle
and Eden, Sam and Ciara, Elias and Milo.

Phobiapedia

All the things we fear the most!

Joel Levy

SCHOLASTIC

Contents

Ophidiophobia, fear of snakes—see page 18.

Mottephobia, fear of moths—see page 50.

Mycophobia, fear of mushrooms and toadstools—see page 63.

Bufonophobia, fear of toads—see page 52.

What is a phobia?

A phobia is an extreme fear of a thing, place, or situation. Sometimes phobias will relate to things that seem genuinely scary, such as snakes or being eaten, but the point about a phobia is that it causes uneasiness even when there is little or no actual danger. For instance, most people know, when looking at a picture of a snake, that the picture itself cannot harm them, but someone with a phobia of snakes may become very upset and afraid. The main symptom of a phobia is anxiety, which can cause shortness of breath, a racing heartbeat, and feelings of panic—not pleasant! Many phobias may seem odd or amusing, but for the sufferer there is nothing funny about it. This book can help us battle our phobias by explaining some of the things we fear the most.

Arachnophobia
Some people do not like spiders, but arachnophobes are really scared of them and will panic if they come into contact with one.

An A–Z of phobias

A

acarophobia *itching or the insects that cause itching*

acerophobia *sourness*

achluophobia *darkness*

acousticophobia *noise*

acrophobia *heights*

aeroacrophobia *open high places*

aerophobia *drafts, swallowing air, or nasty chemicals in the air*

agateophobia *insanity*

agliophobia *pain*

agoraphobia *public or crowded places, leaving a safe place*

agrizoophobia *wild animals*

agyrophobia *crossing the street*

aichmophobia *or* trypanophobia *needles or pointed objects*

ailurophobia *cats*

alektorophobia *chickens*

alliumphobia *garlic*

ambulophobia *walking*

amychophobia *scratches or being scratched*

anablephobia *looking up*

ancraophobia *or* anemophobia *air drafts or wind*

anthrophobia *or* anthophobia *flowers*

antlophobia *floods*

apiphobia *bees*

apotemnophobia *people with amputated arms or legs*

aquaphobia *water*

arachibutyrophobia *peanut butter sticking to the roof of the mouth*

arachnophobia *spiders*

astraphobia *lightning*

astrophobia *stars or space*

asymmetriphobia *things that are not symmetrical*

ataxophobia *disorder or untidiness*

atelophobia *imperfection*

athazagoraphobia *forgetting, or being forgotten or ignored*

atomosophobia *atomic weapons*

automatonophobia *ventriloquists' dummies, waxworks, shop window dummies*

automysophobia *being dirty*

autophobia *or* monophobia *being alone*

aviophobia *or* aviatophobia *flying*

B

bacillophobia *microbes*

bacteriophobia *bacteria*

barophobia *gravity*

bathmophobia *stairs or steep slopes*

bathophobia *depth*

batrachophobia *amphibians, such as frogs, newts, salamanders, etc.*

belonephobia *pins and needles*

bibliophobia *books*

blennophobia *slime*

botanophobia *plants*

brontophobia *thunder and lightning*

bufonophobia *toads*

C

cacophobia *ugliness*

carnophobia *meat*

cheimaphobia *or* cheimatophobia *cold*

chionophobia *snow*

chorophobia *dancing*

chromophobia *or* chromatophobia *colors*

chronomentrophobia *clocks*

cibophobia *or* sitophobia *food or eating*

claustrophobia *confined spaces*

clinophobia *going to bed*

clithrophobia *or* cleithrophobia *being enclosed*

cnidophobia *stings*

coimetrophobia *graveyards*

consecotaleophobia *chopsticks*

An A–Z of phobias

coprophobia   *feces*
coulrophobia   *clowns*
cremnophobia   *precipices, cliff edges, ledges*
cryophobia   *extreme cold, ice, or frost*
cyberphobia   *computers or working on computers*
cynophobia   *dogs or rabies*

D

dendrophobia   *trees*
dinophobia   *dizziness or whirlpools*
doraphobia   *fur or skins of animals*
dystychiphobia   *accidents*

E

ecclesiophobia   *church*
emetophobia   *vomiting*
entomophobia   *insects*
equinophobia *or* hippophobia   *horses*
ereuthophobia   *the color red*

G

geliophobia   *laughter*
geniophobia   *chins*
genuphobia   *knees*
gephyrophobia   *bridges or crossing bridges*
geumaphobia   *flavors or tastes*
graphophobia   *writing or handwriting*

H

haphephobia, hapnophobia, haptephobia,
   or thixophobia   *being touched*
helminthophobia   *being infested with worms*
hemophobia *or* hematophobia   *blood*
herpetophobia   *reptiles or creepy, crawly things*
hexakosioihexekontahexaphobia   *the number 666*
hoplophobia   *guns*
hydrophobia   *water (caused by rabies)*
hygrophobia   *liquids, dampness, or moisture*
hylophobia *or* xylophobia   *forests*

I

iatrophobia   *going to the doctor*
ichthyophobia   *fish*
iophobia   *poison*
isopterophobia   *termites*

K

kinetophobia *or* kinesophobia   *movement or motion*
koniophobia   *dust*
kymophobia   *waves*

L

leukophobia   *the color white*
ligyrophobia   *loud noises*
lilapsophobia   *tornadoes and hurricanes*
limnophobia   *lakes*
lutraphobia   *otters*

M

macrophobia   *long waits*
megalophobia   *large things*
melanophobia   *the color black*
melophobia   *music*
metrophobia   *poetry*
microphobia   *small things*
mottephobia   *moths*
murophobia *or* musophobia   *mice*
mycophobia   *mushrooms*
myrmecophobia   *ants*

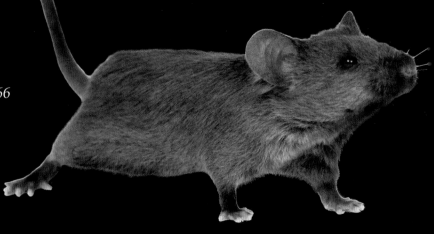

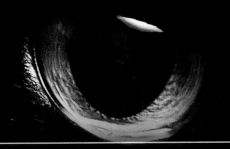
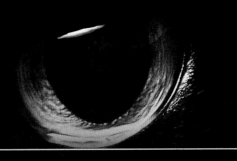

N

necrophobia *corpses*

neophobia *or* kainophobia *new things*

nephophobia *clouds*

noctiphobia *or* nyctophobia *the night*

nosocomephobia *hospitals*

nyctohylophobia *dark wooded areas or forests at night*

O

octophobia *the number eight*

odontophobia *teeth or dental surgery*

odynephobia *pain*

olfactophobia *smells*

ommetaphobia *or* ommatophobia *eyes*

omphalophobia *belly buttons*

oneirophobia *dreams*

ophidiophobia *snakes*

ophthalmophobia *being stared at*

ornithophobia *birds*

ostraconophobia *shellfish*

P

pagophobia *ice or frost*

panophobia *or* pantophobia *everything*

pediculophobia *lice*

pedophobia *children*

phagophobia *swallowing or eating*

phasmophobia *or* spectrophobia *ghosts*

philemaphobia *or* philematophobia *kissing*

phobophobia *phobias*

phonophobia *loud noises*

photophobia *light*

pluviophobia *rain or being rained on*

pnigophobia *or* pnigerophobia *choking or being smothered*

pogonophobia *beards*

pteronophobia *being tickled by feathers*

pupaphobia *puppets*

pyrophobia *fire*

R

ranidaphobia *frogs*

S

sciophobia *or* sciaphobia *shadows*

scoleciphobia *worms*

scotophobia *darkness*

selachophobia *sharks*

selenophobia *the moon*

seplophobia *decaying matter*

spheksophobia *wasps*

stenophobia *narrow things or places*

symmetrophobia *symmetry*

T

taphephobia *or* taphophobia *being buried alive*

taurophobia *bulls*

thalassophobia *the sea*

thanatophobia *or* thantophobia *death or dying*

toxicophobia *or* toxiphobia *poison or being accidentally poisoned*

traumatophobia *injury*

trichopathophobia *or* trichophobia *hair*

triskaidekaphobia *the number 13*

V

vestiphobia *clothing*

X

xanthophobia *the color yellow or the word "yellow"*

xerophobia *dryness*

Z

zoophobia *animals*

Arachnophobia
FEAR of SPIDERS

Arachnophobia (from the Greek *arachne*, meaning "spider," and *phobos*, meaning "fear") is a fear of spiders. It is the most common animal phobia.

Dangerous spiders

Most of the world's spiders are poisonous and more than 200 species worldwide can be dangerous to humans. But most spiders do not have fangs big enough to pierce human skin and deaths from spider bites are very rare. There are many contenders for the world's most venomous (poisonous) spider. The six-eyed sand spider of southern Africa is one—its venom rots the flesh and causes massive bleeding, and there is no antidote (remedy). However, there are no confirmed reports of any human ever having been bitten by one. According to some sources, the Brazilian wandering spider or the Australian Sydney funnel-web spider has the most dangerous venom.

Small and dangerous
The redback spider is only the size of a pea, but is considered one of the most dangerous spiders in Australia.

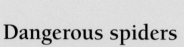

Redback spider

Sydney funnel-web spider

Hungry mates

Some female spiders eat the males after they have mated. The most famous example of this is the black widow spider, although this is only partly true. In one species of black widow, found in the southern hemisphere, the female normally eats the male. In another species, found in North America, the female will sometimes eat the male—but sometimes she lets him go.

Black widow spider

Australia has thousands of species of spiders.

South American tarantula

Wolf spider

Spider eyes
Wolf spiders have eight eyes, which are arranged in three rows. Their strong eyesight helps them find their prey.

Hairy Monsters
Many large, hairy spiders from different parts of the world are known as tarantulas. The original "tarantulas" were wolf spiders from southern Italy, where the town Taranto lent its name to the creatures. They had a painful bite even though they were not highly venomous.

Mexican tarantula
The Mexican red-kneed tarantula may look scary, but it is generally harmless to humans and keeps to itself.

Mexican red-kneed tarantula

Arachnophobes do not like spiders, large or small!

Claustrophobia

FEAR of CONFINED SPACES

Claustrophobia is an uncontrollable fear of confined or very small spaces, from the Latin *claustrum*, meaning a "barrier." It is very common—one in ten people suffer from it at some point. Sometimes small spaces and the fear of being trapped can make you wary, but claustrophobes become anxious even where there is no danger, such as when using elevators or subway trains.

Are you claustrophobic?
Do you feel anxious in a crowd, or have you taken the stairs instead of the elevator because you were frightened of the small space?

In a tight spot

Claustrophobia may be partly inherited. It can also develop as a result of a bad experience early in life, such as riding in an elevator that got stuck, or being locked in a cupboard as a practical joke. The sufferer then becomes afraid of similar situations and starts avoiding them, and this can make the condition worse.

Trapped terror

Not only do cavers travel deep underground, but they often have to squeeze through "sumps"—where a passage is filled to the roof with water—and "crawls"—where a passage requires that the caver go on hands and knees or even lie flat and inch along. In 1925, a crawl claimed the life of caver Floyd Collins. He became trapped 55 feet (17 m) below ground while exploring part of the world's longest cave system—Mammoth Cave in Kentucky. Collins was trapped in the cave for more than two weeks until he died of starvation and thirst.

Low-hanging stalactites make the space seem even smaller!

Cavers' cage

Stalactites and stalagmites create a tight squeeze for cavers. Stalactites hang down and stalagmites point up.

13

Acrophobia

FEAR of HEIGHTS

Acrophobia is a fear of heights (from the Greek *akros*, meaning "peak" or "the highest"). It is often and mistakenly confused with vertigo, a form of dizziness and loss of balance, which is sometimes a symptom of acrophobia and other phobias. People who suffer from acrophobia become anxious and panic-stricken when they look out of windows in tall buildings, when they cross bridges, or even when they stand on a chair!

Angel Falls, Venezuela

Angel Falls

At the top of any acrophobe's list of places not to visit must be the highest waterfall in the world: Angel Falls in Venezuela. The waterfall flows from a flat-topped mountain known as *Auyán-Tepuí* ("Devil Mountain") and plunges 3,212 feet (979 m) into Devil's Canyon. To add to the terror of standing at the top, violent wind, clouds of spray, and slippery mud make it a dangerous place to be. Angel Falls is named after the aviator James Angel, who became the first person to fly over the falls in 1937.

Fear of precipices

Related to acrophobia is cremnophobia, a fear of precipices (very steep places). Cliff tops are particularly scary for cremnophobes. The highest sea cliffs in the world, in Kalaupapa on Molokai island in Hawaii, would be torture for someone with this fear. The cliffs are a mighty 2,000 feet (600 m) high. "Virtual cliffs" can be used to treat acrophobia. Experiments using virtual reality goggles to simulate the experience of being near a cliff edge can help sufferers get over their fear of high places.

Inside the Jin Mao Building, China

The Peak apartment complex, Indonesia

Head for heights
Pictured here (right) are the twin Peak apartments in Jakarta, Indonesia. The twin penthouse apartments are on the 46th to 55th floors—not an ideal place for an acrophobe.

Agoraphobia

FEAR of PUBLIC PLACES

It is often wrongly thought that agoraphobia means "fear of open spaces." The word "agoraphobia" comes from the Greek *agora*, meaning "marketplace." The doctor who came up with the name had been treating patients who became extremely anxious when they were in public places and felt like they could not escape if they needed to. Agoraphobes really suffer from a combination of fears—the fear that they might have a panic attack, and the fear of not being in a safe place.

Agoraphobia is incredibly common—one in every 100 people have severe agoraphobia, and one in eight may experience a mild version. In fact, almost everyone experiences some level of agoraphobia at some point in their lives.

Baby rabbit

Anxious animals

Humans are not the only animals who get nervous out in the wide world. Wild rabbits, for instance, spend much of their time safe in a den, mainly coming out at dusk and dawn when it is light enough to see predators but dark enough not to be seen themselves. Some animals like their homes so much that they carry them around—hermit crabs, for instance, often move into empty sea snail shells and carry them everywhere. When they grow too big for their home they have to find a bigger one, while a chain of smaller crabs lines up behind them to upgrade their own shells.

Staying close
Small animals such as rabbits are always on the lookout for danger and try to stay near their home so that they can run for safety.

On the lookout

The meerkat, part of the mongoose family, is perhaps the most agoraphobic animal. This is hardly surprising, as meerkats have so many predators that around 50 percent of adults are killed every year. Meerkats live in groups or "mobs" of up to 40 individuals. In any group, there is always at least one animal on guard duty, sitting up on its hind legs and looking around for eagles, hawks, jackals, and snakes. If the guard spots something, he or she gives a sharp, shrill call and all the other meerkats dive into the burrow or one of their holes—the quick-escape tunnels that they dig all over the place for safety.

The guard meerkat makes a peeping sound if all is well.

Keeping watch

Meerkats keep guard with an upright position so that they can spot any sign of danger and react before any attack takes place.

17

Ophidiophobia
FEAR of SNAKES

Ophidiophobia (from the Greek *ophis*, meaning "snake") sufferers are scared of snakes. Being nervous about snakes is common, but remember, phobias involve more than just being nervous about or disliking something. Ophidiophobes may be terrified by pictures of snakes, toy snakes, or even just thinking about snakes.

Australian taipan

About 150 species of snake are dangerous to humans.

Rattlesnake

African spitting cobra

What makes snakes so scary?
Lots of people who have never met a snake think that they are slimy, wet, and cold, but in fact this is not true. Snakes have scaly skins that are dry and smooth to the touch. They are cold-blooded but soak up heat from their surroundings, so they usually feel warm.

Is it the fangs?
The most obvious reason for ophidiophobia is that, although many snakes are harmless, others are harmful to humans. Some of these are constrictors—snakes that kill their prey by squeezing it to death—and most are venomous and use poison for attack and defense. But remember, most snakes are shy and hardly ever attack humans, and if they do, they may only inject a small amount of venom in order to escape.

Reticulated python

Deadly bite
The most dangerous venomous snake is probably the carpet viper, found from West Africa to India. It is less toxic than the taipan but probably kills more people than any other species.

Mostly harmless
There are many harmless snakes in the world. In the USA, the vast majority of snakes are not venomous, and a human is more likely to die of an insect bite than of a snake bite. Snake bites are most dangerous in places where antivenom is not available.

Albino Burmese python

Pythons often have colorful, patterned skin.

Ball python

Odontophobia
FEAR of TEETH

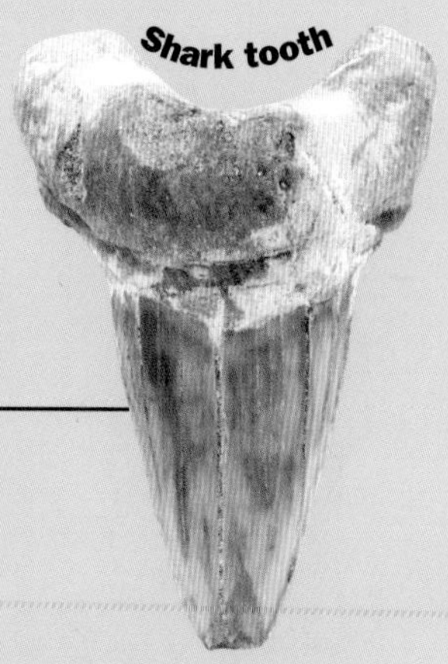

Shark tooth

Great white shark

Odontophobia is a fear of teeth (from the Greek *odon*, meaning "tooth"). It can also mean a fear of having something done to your own teeth, such as going to the dentist. Adult humans have 32 teeth, but some animals have a lot more—and they can be much sharper!

Teeth tell tales

You can tell a lot about an animal from its teeth. Teeth with flat tops are used for grinding tough food, and are mostly found in herbivores (plant-eating animals). Sharp, pointed teeth are used for killing and tearing meat, and are mostly found in carnivores (meat-eating animals).

Big teeth equal big shark

The great white's triangular teeth can be used to estimate the size of the shark. Measure one side of the tooth in inches, and then multiply the number by ten to get the overall length of the creature in feet.

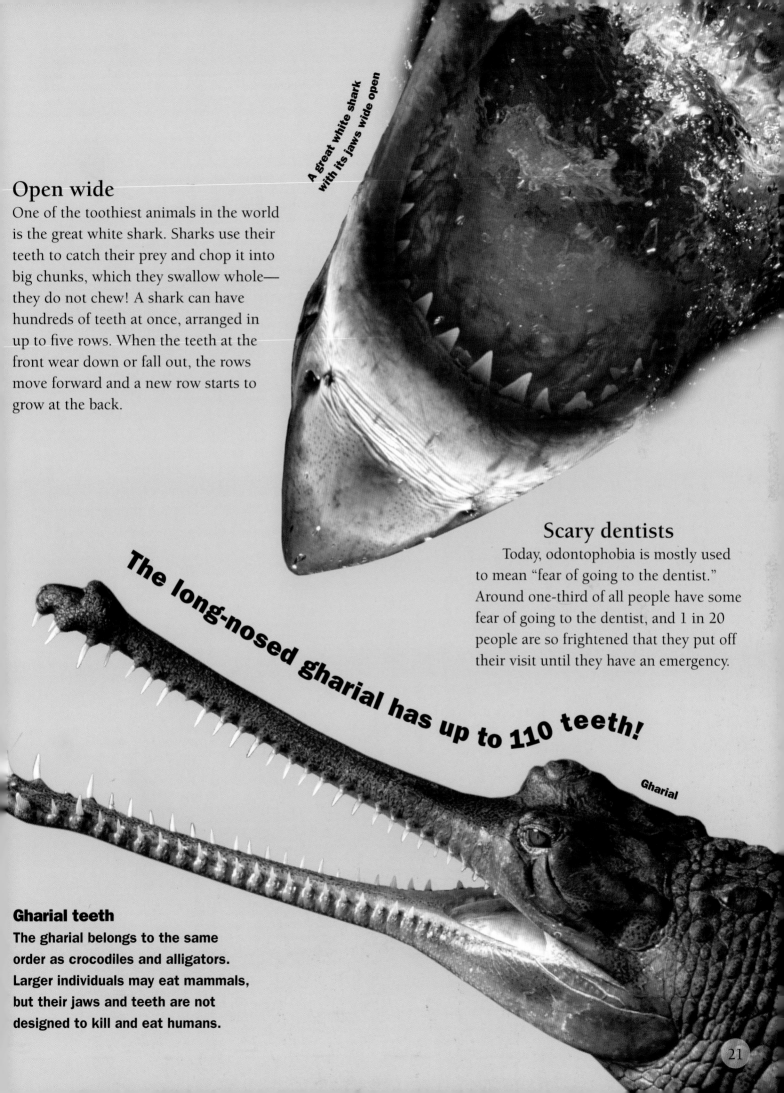

A great white shark with its jaws wide open

Open wide

One of the toothiest animals in the world is the great white shark. Sharks use their teeth to catch their prey and chop it into big chunks, which they swallow whole—they do not chew! A shark can have hundreds of teeth at once, arranged in up to five rows. When the teeth at the front wear down or fall out, the rows move forward and a new row starts to grow at the back.

Scary dentists

Today, odontophobia is mostly used to mean "fear of going to the dentist." Around one-third of all people have some fear of going to the dentist, and 1 in 20 people are so frightened that they put off their visit until they have an emergency.

The long-nosed gharial has up to 110 teeth!

Gharial

Gharial teeth

The gharial belongs to the same order as crocodiles and alligators. Larger individuals may eat mammals, but their jaws and teeth are not designed to kill and eat humans.

Emetophobia
FEAR of VOMITING

Emetophobia comes from the Greek *emein*, meaning "to vomit." At first glance, this phobia may seem pretty sensible—there is no doubt that vomit is nasty stuff. Typical human vomit consists of partially digested food, spit, acidic stomach juices, and maybe even nastier stuff such as blood and bile! It is not surprising that most people do not like vomit and vomiting. Emetophobia, however, is much more serious than simple dislike.

Staying healthy at all costs

Emetophobes are so afraid that they might vomit, or that they might see other people vomit, that they take extreme steps to avoid the possibility. Some emetophobes avoid small children, stay away from parties, and obsessively wash food before eating it.

Take cover!

Humans generally vomit because their bodies react automatically to get rid of certain substances, such as poisons, that might be harmful to their health. But some animals use vomit as a form of defense against predators.

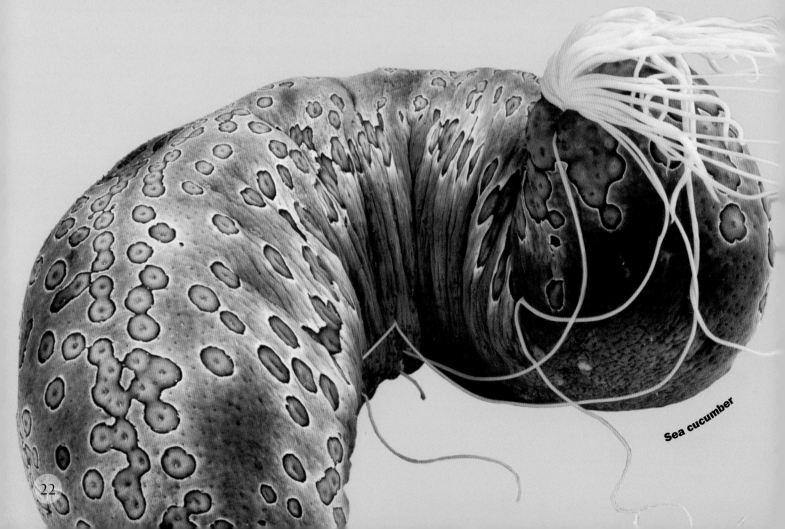

Sea cucumber

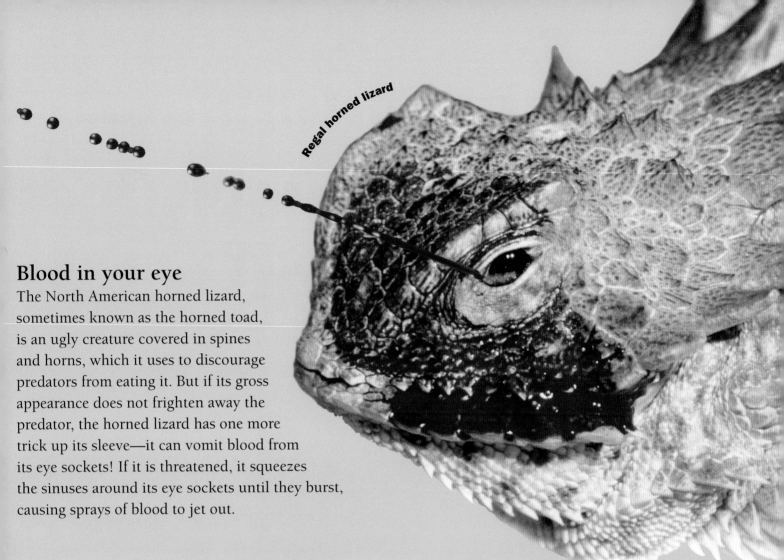

Regal horned lizard

Blood in your eye

The North American horned lizard, sometimes known as the horned toad, is an ugly creature covered in spines and horns, which it uses to discourage predators from eating it. But if its gross appearance does not frighten away the predator, the horned lizard has one more trick up its sleeve—it can vomit blood from its eye sockets! If it is threatened, it squeezes the sinuses around its eye sockets until they burst, causing sprays of blood to jet out.

Sea cucumber squirt
A sea cucumber squirts out its guts in order to stop or attack predators.

Lizard blood
The blood that the lizard shoots out contains nasty, foul-tasting chemicals.

Bottom burps

The sea cucumber seems like a harmless and fairly boring creature. Related to the sea urchin, it is a slow-moving animal that feeds on rotting plant matter on the seabed. Sea cucumbers are usually around 8 inches (20 cm) long, but the tiger tail sea cucumber can grow to 6.5 feet (2 m)—longer than most adult humans. The most startling thing about this animal is its defense mechanism. If threatened by predators, such as fish, the sea cucumber will do a sort of vomit from its backside, blasting its internal organs toward the predator.

Sea cucumbers attack by shooting out poisonous threads!

Brontophobia

FEAR of THUNDER and LIGHTNING

The word "brontophobia" comes from the Greek for thunder, *bronte*. The fear of thunder usually goes hand in hand with astraphobia, the fear of lightning. These phobias are particularly common in children.

Deadly storms

Thunderstorms are loud and scary and they can also be quite dangerous. In the USA, an average of 58 people a year die from being struck by lightning. Only floods cause more weather-related deaths.

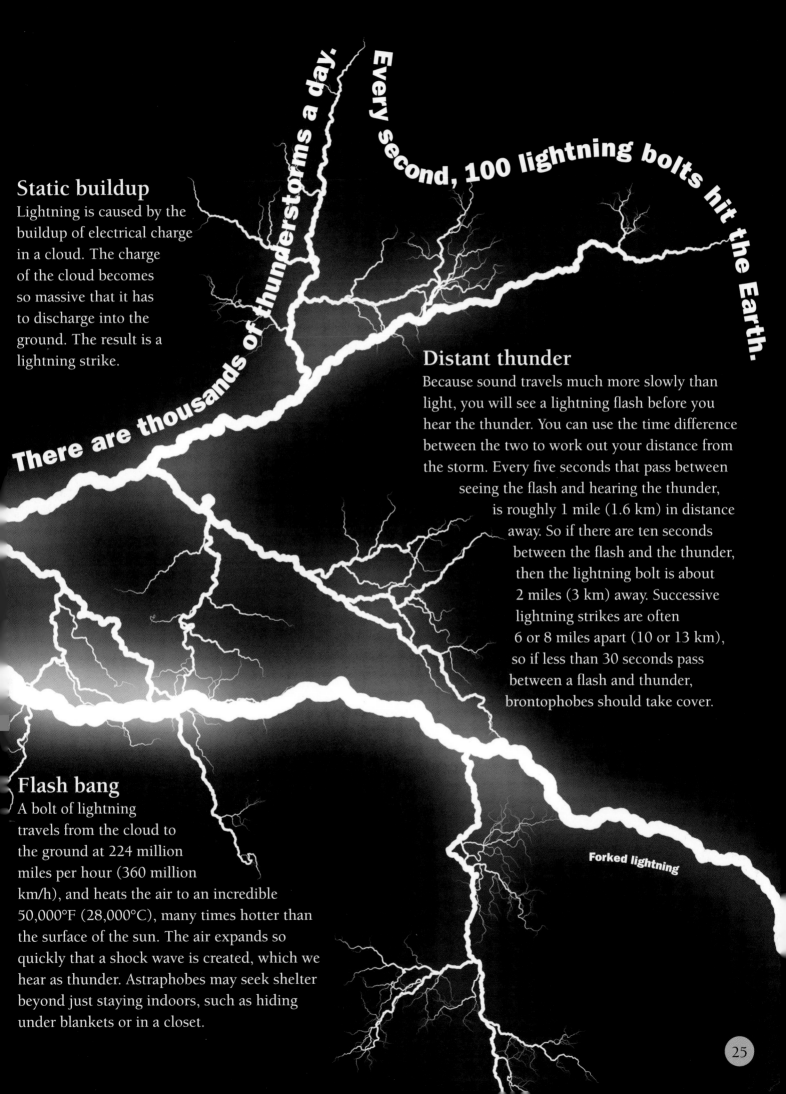

Static buildup

Lightning is caused by the buildup of electrical charge in a cloud. The charge of the cloud becomes so massive that it has to discharge into the ground. The result is a lightning strike.

Distant thunder

Because sound travels much more slowly than light, you will see a lightning flash before you hear the thunder. You can use the time difference between the two to work out your distance from the storm. Every five seconds that pass between seeing the flash and hearing the thunder, is roughly 1 mile (1.6 km) in distance away. So if there are ten seconds between the flash and the thunder, then the lightning bolt is about 2 miles (3 km) away. Successive lightning strikes are often 6 or 8 miles apart (10 or 13 km), so if less than 30 seconds pass between a flash and thunder, brontophobes should take cover.

Flash bang

A bolt of lightning travels from the cloud to the ground at 224 million miles per hour (360 million km/h), and heats the air to an incredible 50,000°F (28,000°C), many times hotter than the surface of the sun. The air expands so quickly that a shock wave is created, which we hear as thunder. Astraphobes may seek shelter beyond just staying indoors, such as hiding under blankets or in a closet.

Forked lightning

25

Hemophobia
FEAR of BLOOD

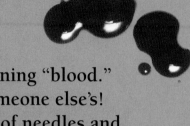

The word "hemophobia" comes from the Greek root *aima*, meaning "blood." Hemophobes cannot stand the sight of blood—their own or someone else's! This phobia often goes hand in hand with trypanophobia (fear of needles and sharp, pointed things) and traumatophobia (fear of injuries). For hemophobes, fainting is a common reaction to the sight of blood, and this can be dangerous, as injuries can occur. Hemophobes find it hard to visit doctors and dislike getting shots.

Why fear your own blood?

Some experts think that hemophobia is a problem because many people hardly ever see blood in their day-to-day lives, so they do not know how to deal with it when they do. The natural world is very different: Blood is everywhere. It is especially important for animals that use blood as a food source.

Blood suckers

Some animals love blood. Mosquitoes are a major global health hazard because they spread many blood-borne diseases, including malaria, which kills more than a million people a year. However, there are a lot of wrong ideas about mosquitoes. For instance, mosquitoes do not bite—they use their needlelike noses like syringes to suck out the blood. They do not live on blood, either. Mainly, they feed on sugary fluids, or nectar, from plants. Only female mosquitoes drink blood when they are producing eggs.

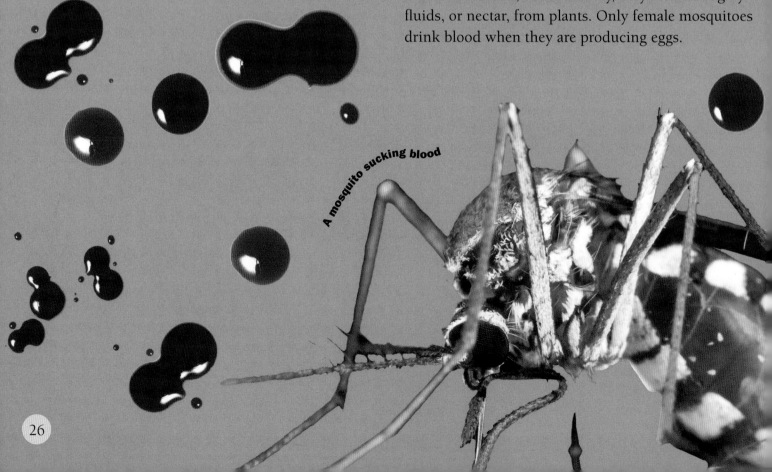

A mosquito sucking blood

Pleased to eat you

Vampire bats are the only mammals that live exclusively on blood. They feed mostly on sleeping cattle and horses. They only occasionally bite humans, but this does not stop people from being afraid of them and what they can do. Using a special heat sensor on its nose, the bat is able to locate a blood vessel close to the skin and bite into it.

A vampire bat hangs upside down.

Vampire bats live in colonies of around 100. A colony can drink the blood of 25 cows in a year.

Belly full of blood

In the darkest hours of the night, vampire bats leave the caves where they live, in colonies of 100 to 1,000 animals, and fly out to feed. Each bat feeds for up to 30 minutes and can drink its own weight in blood.

Cynophobia

FEAR of DOGS and RABIES

Dogs are supposed to be our friends, but many people are terrified of them. People who suffer from cynophobia (from the Greek word *kyon*, meaning "dog") cannot bear to be near dogs and may have a panic attack if one approaches them. For these people, the bad news is that there are a lot of dogs in the world.

Watch for signs

A dog bares its sharp teeth.

Natural aggression

Where does the fear of dogs come from? Dogs can actually be extremely dangerous—although deaths from dog attacks are incredibly rare, bites are relatively common. In the USA, 4.7 million people get bitten each year. Most of these are not serious enough to need a visit to the doctor.

Growling rottweiler

Dogs and rabies
People suffering from cynophobia may not have a fear of dogs, but may fear the disease rabies. Dogs contract rabies by being bitten by an infected animal. A dog with rabies can be extremely dangerous.

of aggression.

Danger signals
Any dog can be dangerous if it feels threatened. Watch out for the danger signs: growling, raised hackles (the hairs on the dog's back), bared teeth, wrinkling of the nose, and a tail that is stiff or vibrating (not wagging). Do not run! Fold your arms, turn away, and do not make eye contact.

Dog with its mouth wide open

29

Aichmophobia

FEAR of POINTY THINGS

Aichmophobia, from the Greek *aichme* ("point"), is a fear of anything sharp or pointed, from needles to umbrella tips! It is closely related to trypanophobia (the fear of injections), which is an extremely common phobia that affects at least one in ten people, sometimes resulting in fainting. It is one of the few phobias that can, in rare circumstances, be fatal.

Shot full of fear

Trypanophobia usually begins with an automatic reaction of the body to getting stuck with a needle. The sufferer has no conscious control of the body. The blood vessels suddenly get wider and this causes a dramatic loss of blood pressure, which in turn causes fainting.

Trypanophobes fear the body's reaction to needles.

The stinger of a common wasp

Wasp and bee stingers

Many wasp species have egg-laying tubes, called "ovipositors." These tubes can be very long and look very sharp—just like an enormous stinger. The ichneumon wasp's 3-inch (7.6-cm) long ovipositor is a trypanophobe's nightmare.

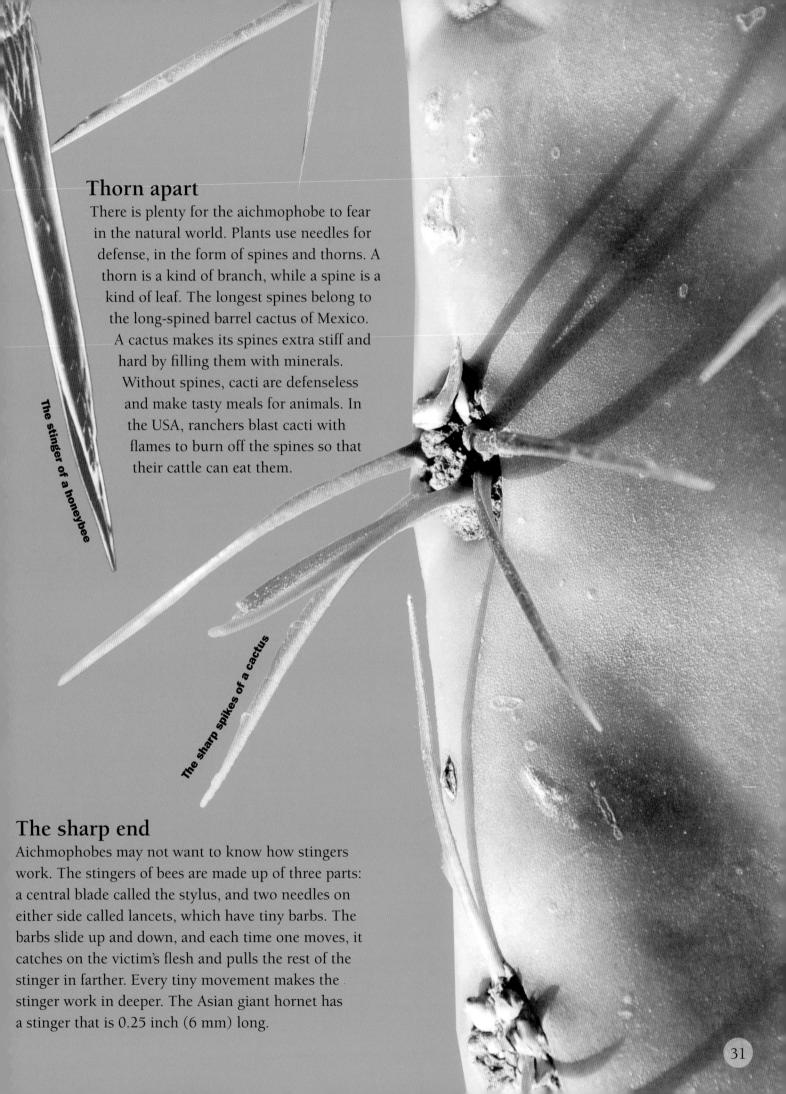

Thorn apart

There is plenty for the aichmophobe to fear in the natural world. Plants use needles for defense, in the form of spines and thorns. A thorn is a kind of branch, while a spine is a kind of leaf. The longest spines belong to the long-spined barrel cactus of Mexico. A cactus makes its spines extra stiff and hard by filling them with minerals. Without spines, cacti are defenseless and make tasty meals for animals. In the USA, ranchers blast cacti with flames to burn off the spines so that their cattle can eat them.

The stinger of a honeybee

The sharp spikes of a cactus

The sharp end

Aichmophobes may not want to know how stingers work. The stingers of bees are made up of three parts: a central blade called the stylus, and two needles on either side called lancets, which have tiny barbs. The barbs slide up and down, and each time one moves, it catches on the victim's flesh and pulls the rest of the stinger in farther. Every tiny movement makes the stinger work in deeper. The Asian giant hornet has a stinger that is 0.25 inch (6 mm) long.

Nyctophobia
FEAR of the DARK

Ghost-faced bat

Nyctophobia, from the Greek *nyx*, meaning "night," is a fear of darkness. It is also sometimes known as scotophobia. Nyctophobia is common in children but most grow out of it. Some adults, however, are so frightened of the dark that they will not leave the house at night and must sleep with a night-light on. Although nyctophobia is an extreme reaction, darkness is linked to fear and anxiety for almost all humans.

Nocturnal wonders

Humans are diurnal, which means that we are active during the day and rest at night. Nighttime can seem alien and dangerous, full of creepy noises, spooky shadows, and weird and wonderful creatures that only come out at night (called nocturnal animals).

Night creatures use special

Barn owl

The bright eyes of a cat

Small elephant hawk moth

Hawk moth
This species has highly developed night vision and can even see colors in low light.

senses in the dark.

Danger in the night

To increase their chances of survival, early humans most likely formed social groups and were active during the day. That way they could always have someone on the lookout for danger. At night, they would retreat to caves and sheltered places to make it harder for predators to sneak up on them.

Blood-sucking owls

This prehistoric link between darkness and danger is probably why the night has always been associated with evil and the supernatural, and why creatures that are active at night also have this connection. Many cultures have linked owls to ghosts and evil spirits. The barn owl, a widespread species, has also been called the ghost owl, death owl, and demon owl, thanks to its eerie cry and the way it glides silently out of the darkness.

Lesser nighthawk

Nighthawk
This swallowlike bird is active at night, mainly toward dawn and dusk, when it catches insects while flying.

Night vision

The main challenge for nocturnal creatures is the fact that it is dark. Some nocturnal animals rely on other senses. Bats make high-pitched squeaks and pick up the echoes with their super-sensitive ears. Other animals, such as owls and cats, have eyes that can pick up even the faintest light.

Ornithophobia

FEAR of BIRDS

Ornithophobes have plenty to fear, because there are more than 9,000 species of birds in the world! But are birds really all that terrifying? Anyone who has been in a room with a trapped pigeon knows that the panicked, flapping wings and messy droppings can be nerve-racking for the calmest person.

Vulture

Giant flocks

Fortunately for ornithophobes, mass bird attacks are rare. Attacks on people usually involve just one or two birds—this is known as mobbing, and it's not uncommon. Birds typically gather into huge flocks for reasons other than attacking. Species such as starlings gather together for protection. In Denmark, a phenomenon called the Black Sun is caused by flocks of more than a million starlings swirling in the sky. Now extinct, passenger pigeons in North America used to travel in flocks that blotted out the sky continuously for days at a time, causing a dark, scary scene in the sky that would be daunting for anyone.

Vicious vultures
Vultures are birds of prey that usually feed on animals that are already dead.

White dove

Harmless birds
Even the most calm and harmless-looking birds can make an ornithophobe panic and feel unwell.

A flock of birds can be daunting.

Thunderbirds
Ornithophobes should be grateful that one of the world's largest living flying birds, the Andean condor, with a wingspan up to 10.5 feet (3.2 m), is small compared to the largest bird that ever lived—the teratorn. With its massive wingspan of 21 feet (6.4 m), the teratorn was a prehistoric monster. It was almost the size of a light aircraft—a nightmare for the ornithophobe!

Blackbirds gather together.

35

Selachophobia
FEAR of SHARKS

Most people would be terrified of a shark if they met
one in the water, but selachophobes can barely look at
a picture of a shark, and some may be too scared to
go in the water even in parts of the world where
the chances of meeting a shark are small.

Whale shark

Gentle giants

Shark attacks are rare—about
60–100 occur per year and only a
handful of people are killed. The largest
shark of all is the whale shark, at 40 feet (12 m)
long. Reassuringly, it is harmless to humans,
feeding only on fish.

Great whites

The great white is responsible for many deadly shark
attacks. They can reach up to two-thirds the size of
a school bus and can sense drops of blood in the
water from up to 3 miles (5 km) away, and swim
at 15 miles per hour (24 km/h).

Megamouth diet

The megamouth shark (right) was only discovered in the 1970s, despite being up to 17 feet (5.2 m) long. Although it is large, this big guy has a dainty diet of small fish and shrimp.

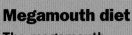

Megamouth shark

These monsters of the deep are harmless.

The whale shark sucks prey into its massive mouth.

Nowhere to hide

Selachophobes might think they are safe when swimming in a river, but the most dangerous of all sharks, the aggressive and vicious bull shark, which can be up to 11.5 feet (3.5 m) long, often swims up rivers. Bull sharks have been found thousands of miles inland and can leap rapids (fast currents), enabling them to reach lakes. Whereas great whites tend to "sample bite," taking a chunk out of a human and then swimming away, bull sharks stay and finish the job.

Fight back

Selachophobes should be prepared to fight if they come across a shark. Experts say that you should never play dead. Instead, hit the shark on the nose and target the gills and the eyes, which are the most sensitive parts of the shark.

Aquaphobia
FEAR of WATER

Aquaphobia sufferers range from people who are afraid of deep water but will go swimming, to people who will not even take a bath. The most common form of aquaphobia is a fear of putting one's head under the water, or more specifically one's nose and ears. This fear is often seen in children but most grow out of it.

Even calm, still water can be daunting for aquaphobia sufferers.

Normally the name for a phobia is formed from the Greek word for the subject of the phobia, in which case fear of water would be "hydrophobia." However, this term is used by doctors to describe a specific symptom of rabies, so to avoid confusion, the Latin word for water—*aqua*—is used instead. A related fear is thalassophobia, fear of the sea.

A boat floats in still water.

Raining and pouring

Where is the worst place in the world for an aquaphobe to live? It might be Waialeale in Hawaii, which has an average of 335 rainy days a year. Or it could be the tiny Pacific Island nation of Tuvalu, at most just 15 feet (4.5 m) above sea level. Aquaphobes should head for Arica in Chile, which has an average of only one rainy day every six years.

Big, fat raindrops can be intimidating.

Even a movie can trigger an aquaphobic reaction.

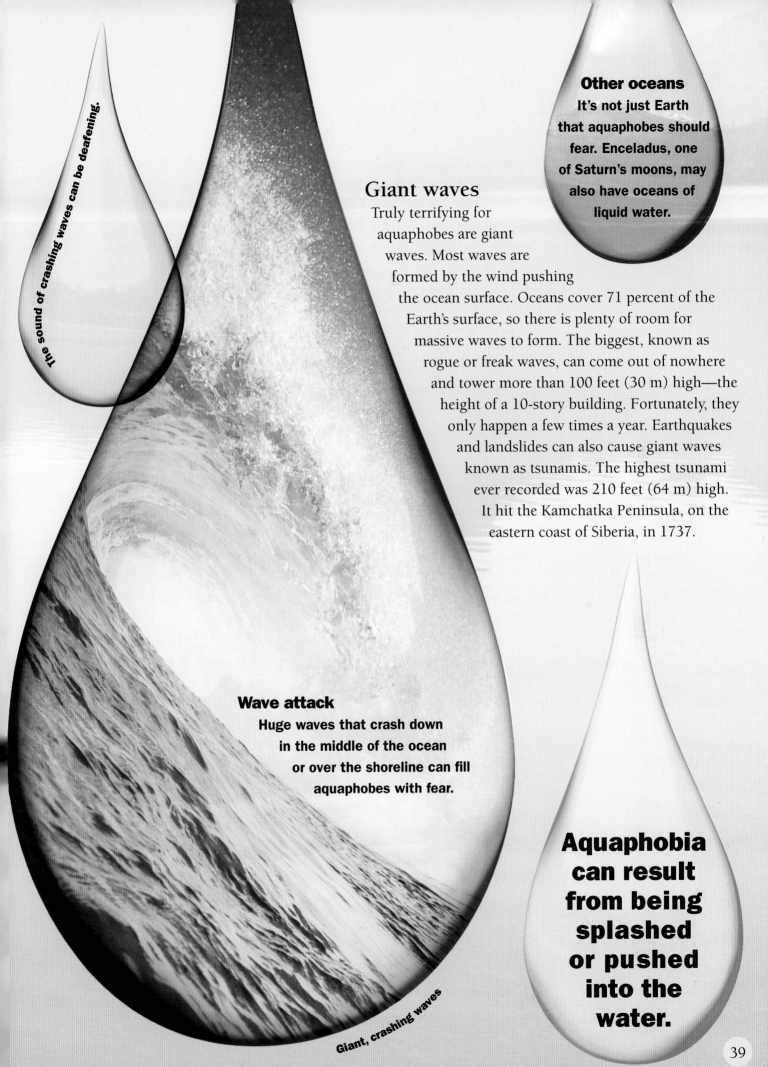

The sound of crashing waves can be deafening.

Other oceans
It's not just Earth that aquaphobes should fear. Enceladus, one of Saturn's moons, may also have oceans of liquid water.

Giant waves

Truly terrifying for aquaphobes are giant waves. Most waves are formed by the wind pushing the ocean surface. Oceans cover 71 percent of the Earth's surface, so there is plenty of room for massive waves to form. The biggest, known as rogue or freak waves, can come out of nowhere and tower more than 100 feet (30 m) high—the height of a 10-story building. Fortunately, they only happen a few times a year. Earthquakes and landslides can also cause giant waves known as tsunamis. The highest tsunami ever recorded was 210 feet (64 m) high. It hit the Kamchatka Peninsula, on the eastern coast of Siberia, in 1737.

Wave attack
Huge waves that crash down in the middle of the ocean or over the shoreline can fill aquaphobes with fear.

Aquaphobia can result from being splashed or pushed into the water.

Giant, crashing waves

39

Apiphobia and Spheksophobia

FEAR of BEES and FEAR of WASPS

Wasps kill pests.

Yellow jacket wasp

Bees and wasps are among the most dangerous animals in the world, in terms of the number of human deaths caused. In the USA, around 100 people die each year from being stung, because insect stings can trigger an allergic reaction called an anaphylactic shock, which leads to suffocation and heart failure. However, only a small percentage of people react badly to a sting and they can carry medication with them to combat the effect.

Be afraid....

If wasps and bees are so dangerous, why isn't everyone apiphobic (from the Greek *apis*, meaning "bee") or spheksophobic (from the Greek *sphekes*, meaning "wasp")? Even in a country full of poisonous snakes, such as the USA, you are more likely to die from a bee sting than a snakebite. And an anaphylactic shock strikes with lethal speed.

Nature's helpers

In fact there is no need to panic if a wasp or bee approaches, as it is very rare for one to sting unless provoked. The truth is that the world needs bees and wasps. Not only do bees make honey, they also carry pollen between plants, and farmers rely on bees to pollinate their crops, while wasps kill crop pests.

Bees pollinate crops.

Tawny mining bee

Killer bee

Black and yellow stripes warn off predators.

Killer bees and giant hornets

Not all bees and wasps help humans,
however. The Africanized honeybee,
also known as the killer bee, is an aggressive
species that has invaded much of the Americas.
Killer bee colonies will attack any "threat"
within 100 feet (30 m) and chase people
for up to 0.25 mile (400 m)!

Bee venom can be used to help arthritis.

European hornet

Protect your eyes

Killer bees are slow
enough for most people to outrun, so the best
thing to do if you are attacked is to protect
your eyes, cover your mouth, and run away in a
straight line! Do not try to hide underwater, as
a swarm of bees will wait for you to resurface.

Entomophobia
FEAR of INSECTS

The word "entomophobia" comes from the Greek word *entomon*, meaning "segmented," a reference to the way insects' bodies are organized. It is a fear of insects and is common—perhaps this is not surprising given the number and variety of creepy-crawlies in the world! If you put all the insects on the planet together, they would weigh more than all other animals combined.

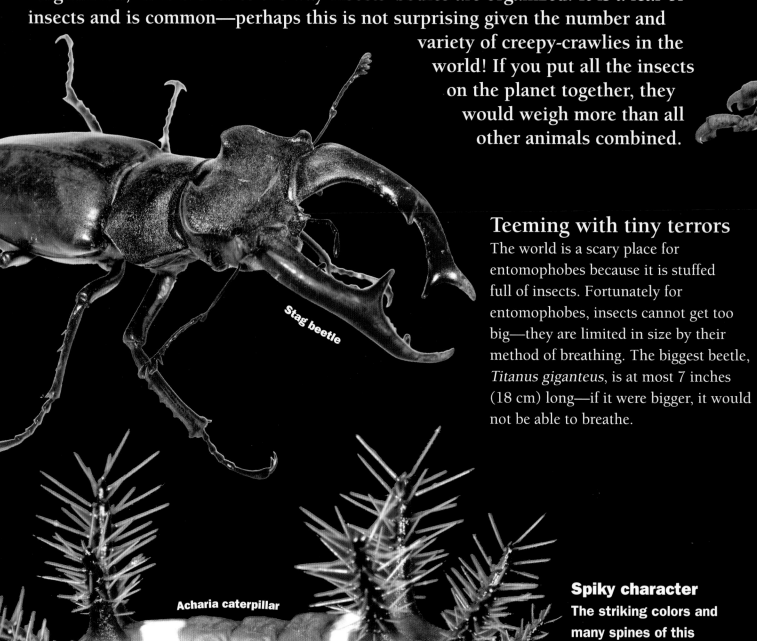

Stag beetle

Teeming with tiny terrors

The world is a scary place for entomophobes because it is stuffed full of insects. Fortunately for entomophobes, insects cannot get too big—they are limited in size by their method of breathing. The biggest beetle, *Titanus giganteus*, is at most 7 inches (18 cm) long—if it were bigger, it would not be able to breathe.

Acharia caterpillar

Spiky character
The striking colors and many spines of this Acharia caterpillar warn predators to stay away.

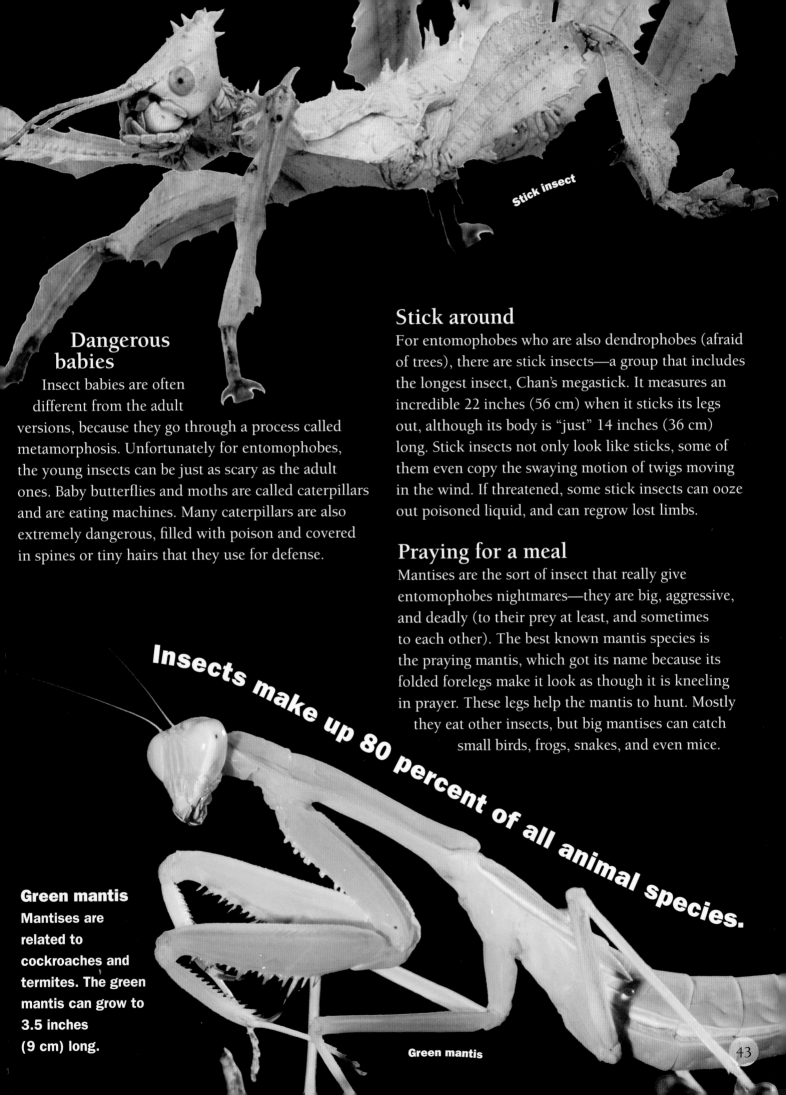

Stick insect

Dangerous babies

Insect babies are often different from the adult versions, because they go through a process called metamorphosis. Unfortunately for entomophobes, the young insects can be just as scary as the adult ones. Baby butterflies and moths are called caterpillars and are eating machines. Many caterpillars are also extremely dangerous, filled with poison and covered in spines or tiny hairs that they use for defense.

Stick around

For entomophobes who are also dendrophobes (afraid of trees), there are stick insects—a group that includes the longest insect, Chan's megastick. It measures an incredible 22 inches (56 cm) when it sticks its legs out, although its body is "just" 14 inches (36 cm) long. Stick insects not only look like sticks, some of them even copy the swaying motion of twigs moving in the wind. If threatened, some stick insects can ooze out poisoned liquid, and can regrow lost limbs.

Praying for a meal

Mantises are the sort of insect that really give entomophobes nightmares—they are big, aggressive, and deadly (to their prey at least, and sometimes to each other). The best known mantis species is the praying mantis, which got its name because its folded forelegs make it look as though it is kneeling in prayer. These legs help the mantis to hunt. Mostly they eat other insects, but big mantises can catch small birds, frogs, snakes, and even mice.

Insects make up 80 percent of all animal species.

Green mantis
Mantises are related to cockroaches and termites. The green mantis can grow to 3.5 inches (9 cm) long.

Green mantis

Clithrophobia

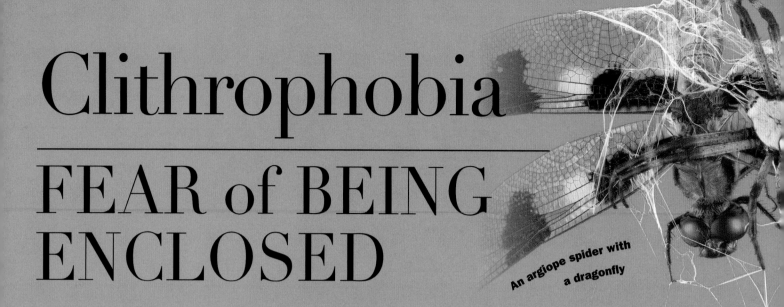

FEAR of BEING ENCLOSED

Clithro- or cleithrophobia, from the Greek *kleithron*, meaning "bolt," as in "lock," is a morbid fear of being locked in, enclosed, confined, or trapped in a small space. It is a type of claustrophobia. The clithrophobe's worst nightmare is to be buried alive, a horrifying scenario!

An argiope spider with a dragonfly

Tasty bite

An argiope spider (above) injecting its venom into its captured dragonfly prey before it wraps the insect in silk—causing a drawn-out death.

Getting trapped and enduring a long and agonizing end are fears for the clithrophobe. Boa constrictors, pythons, and anacondas are the animals that the clithrophobe probably least wants to meet. Instead of relying on venom to immobilize and kill their prey, these large snakes use their long, powerful, muscular bodies to surround and crush other animals. Once the prey has stopped struggling, the snake unhinges its jaws and swallows the animal whole—sometimes the animal is still alive.

Mighty constrictors

The longest snake in captivity, according to the *Guinness Book of Records*, was a reticulated python in the Columbus Zoo and Aquarium, in Ohio. It was an impressive 24 feet (7 m) long. In 2008, researchers discovered fossils of a snake they called *Titanoboa*, which was 45 feet (14 m) long—about the length of a bus—and lived in the rain forest of northeast Colombia. It was so huge that it could have swallowed a crocodile.

Egg-eating snakes swallow their meals whole.

African egg-eating snake swallowing an egg

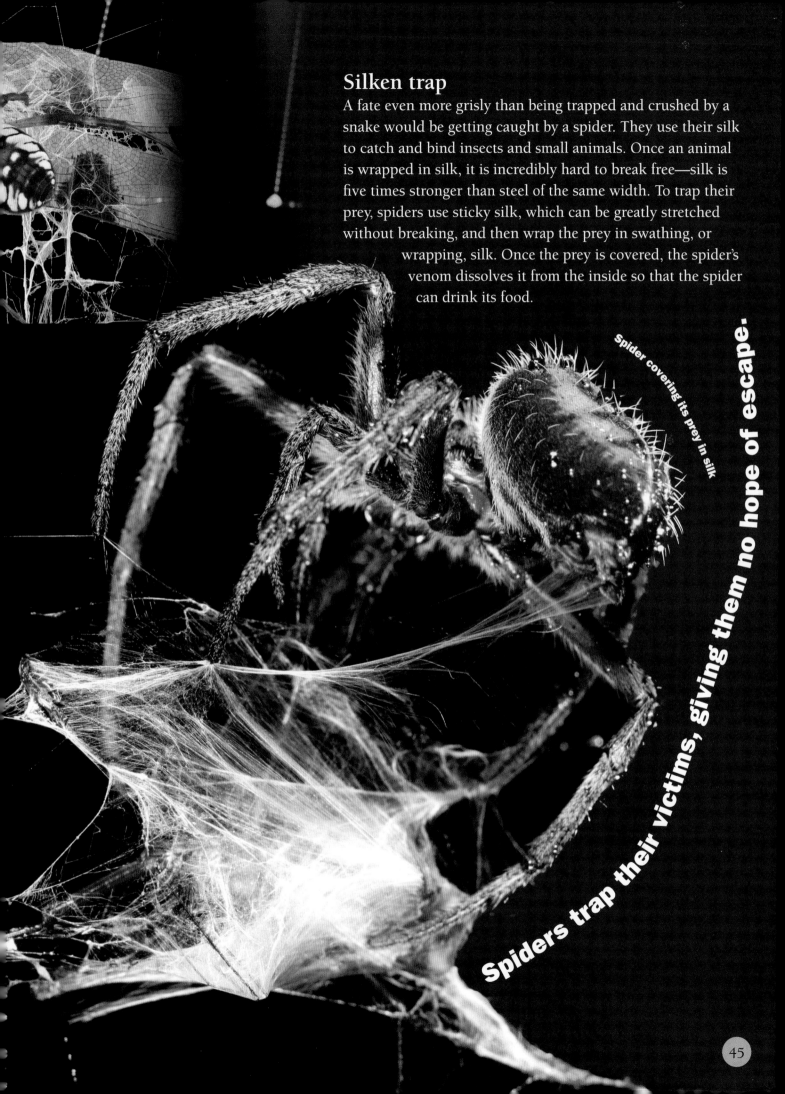

Silken trap

A fate even more grisly than being trapped and crushed by a snake would be getting caught by a spider. They use their silk to catch and bind insects and small animals. Once an animal is wrapped in silk, it is incredibly hard to break free—silk is five times stronger than steel of the same width. To trap their prey, spiders use sticky silk, which can be greatly stretched without breaking, and then wrap the prey in swathing, or wrapping, silk. Once the prey is covered, the spider's venom dissolves it from the inside so that the spider can drink its food.

Spider covering its prey in silk

Spiders trap their victims, giving them no hope of escape.

Musophobia

FEAR of RATS and MICE

Musophobia, also known as murophobia, is a morbid fear of mice and rats. Perhaps not surprisingly, it is one of the most common phobias. Mice and rats are pests closely connected with humans—where there are people, there will be rodents.

A group of baby mice

Age-old fear

Musophobia has historical roots stretching back to the Middle Ages and far beyond. As soon as humans began to store food in one place (rather than hunting and gathering it as they moved around), mice and rats moved in to help themselves.

Mouse explosion

A female mouse can produce 25 to 60 babies a year, and the females are ready to have babies after just six to ten weeks.

Rats and mice can spread disease and ruin food.

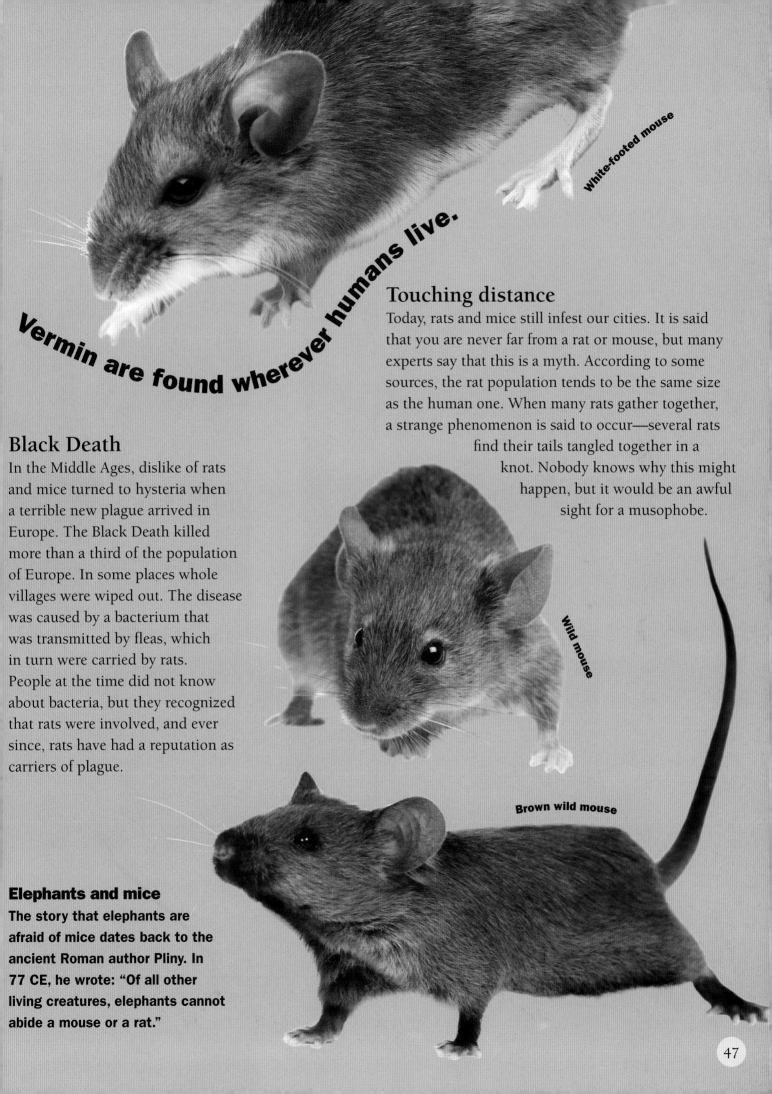

White-footed mouse

Vermin are found wherever humans live.

Touching distance
Today, rats and mice still infest our cities. It is said that you are never far from a rat or mouse, but many experts say that this is a myth. According to some sources, the rat population tends to be the same size as the human one. When many rats gather together, a strange phenomenon is said to occur—several rats find their tails tangled together in a knot. Nobody knows why this might happen, but it would be an awful sight for a musophobe.

Black Death
In the Middle Ages, dislike of rats and mice turned to hysteria when a terrible new plague arrived in Europe. The Black Death killed more than a third of the population of Europe. In some places whole villages were wiped out. The disease was caused by a bacterium that was transmitted by fleas, which in turn were carried by rats. People at the time did not know about bacteria, but they recognized that rats were involved, and ever since, rats have had a reputation as carriers of plague.

Wild mouse

Brown wild mouse

Elephants and mice
The story that elephants are afraid of mice dates back to the ancient Roman author Pliny. In 77 CE, he wrote: "Of all other living creatures, elephants cannot abide a mouse or a rat."

Clinophobia

FEAR of GOING TO BED

The word "clinophobia" comes from the Greek *klinein*, meaning "to incline," that is, to lean back or lie down. Normally a bed is comforting and is a place where you can rest and relax, but for clinophobes the prospect of going to bed is worrying and even terrifying—not because of the bed itself, but because of what might happen while they are asleep. Clinophobia can cause insomnia (the inability to sleep), and this in turn can lead to serious health problems.

Greater false vampire bat

Time for bed
So what are clinophobes afraid of? Children may be anxious about bed-wetting, but adult clinophobes tend to be scared of something much, much worse—that they might never wake up. Fear of dying while they are asleep is what keeps most clinophobes awake.

Nighttime creatures
Creatures that come out at night, such as bats, are sometimes considered disturbing and often increase fear for the clinophobe.

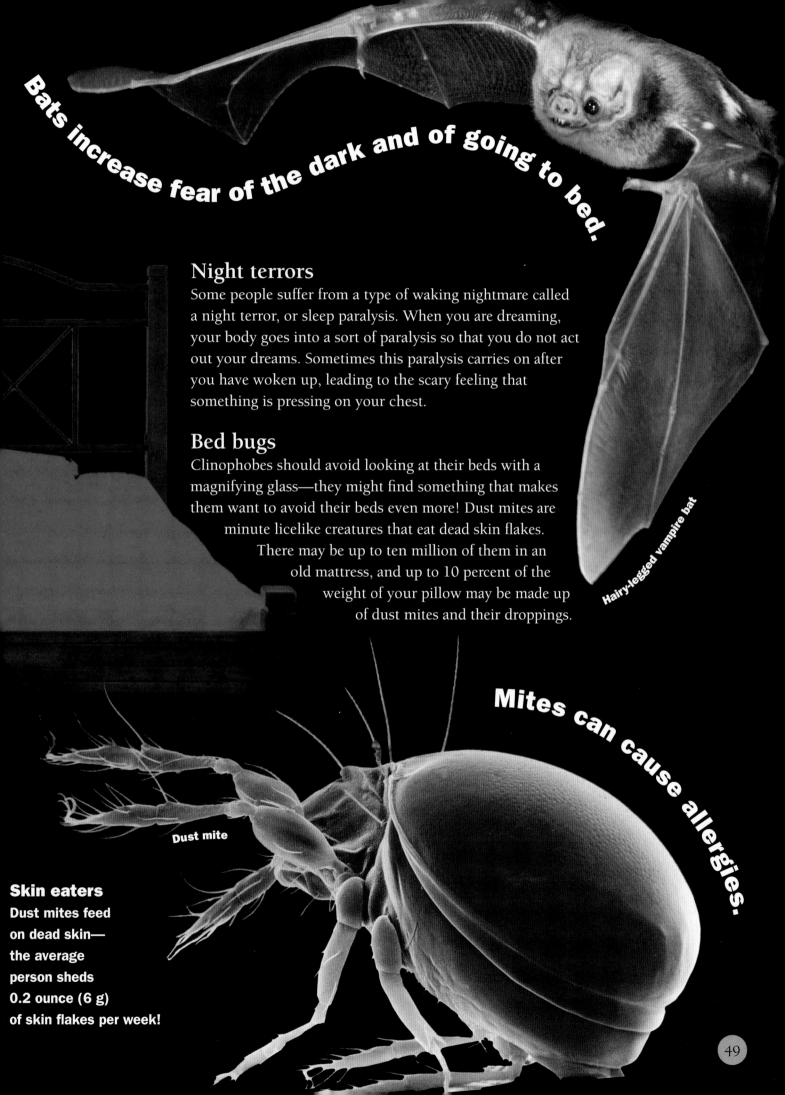

Night terrors

Some people suffer from a type of waking nightmare called a night terror, or sleep paralysis. When you are dreaming, your body goes into a sort of paralysis so that you do not act out your dreams. Sometimes this paralysis carries on after you have woken up, leading to the scary feeling that something is pressing on your chest.

Bed bugs

Clinophobes should avoid looking at their beds with a magnifying glass—they might find something that makes them want to avoid their beds even more! Dust mites are minute licelike creatures that eat dead skin flakes. There may be up to ten million of them in an old mattress, and up to 10 percent of the weight of your pillow may be made up of dust mites and their droppings.

Hairy-legged vampire bat

Mites can cause allergies.

Dust mite

Skin eaters
Dust mites feed on dead skin—the average person sheds 0.2 ounce (6 g) of skin flakes per week!

Mottephobia

FEAR of MOTHS

From the German *motte*, meaning "moth," mottephobia is the fear of moths. What is it about moths that scares so many people? A combination of appearance, habits, and the place of the moth in mythology are probably to blame.

Furry horrors
Most butterflies are colorful and fly around in the day, whereas moths are mostly nocturnal (come out at night), and tend to be more furry and less brightly colored. Because they are night creatures, moths are linked with death and darkness in many countries.

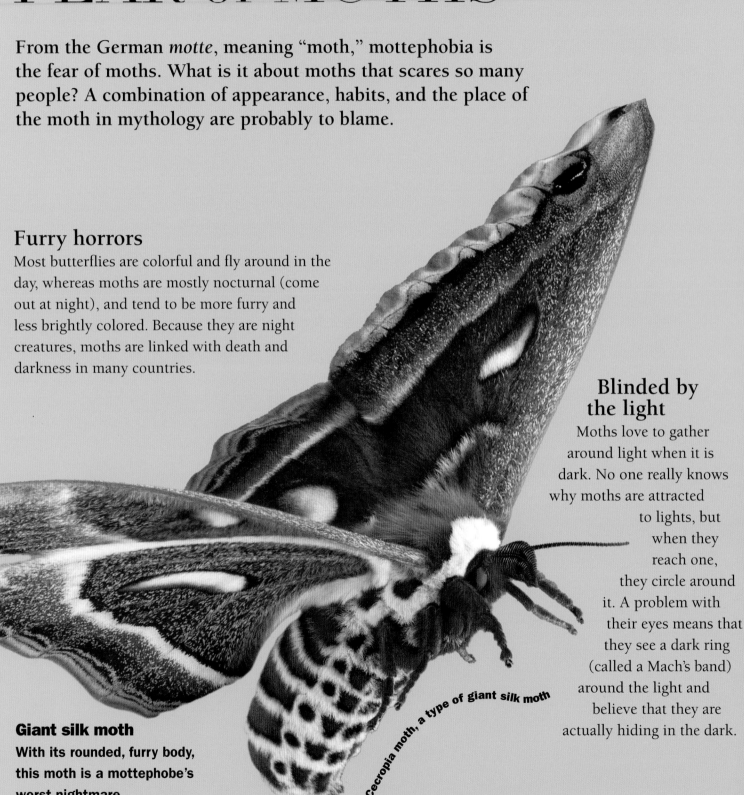

Cecropia moth, a type of giant silk moth

Blinded by the light
Moths love to gather around light when it is dark. No one really knows why moths are attracted to lights, but when they reach one, they circle around it. A problem with their eyes means that they see a dark ring (called a Mach's band) around the light and believe that they are actually hiding in the dark.

Giant silk moth
With its rounded, furry body, this moth is a mottephobe's worst nightmare.

Many moths have strange wing patterns.

Giant silkworm moth

Elephant hawk moth

Heaven scent

Mottephobes hate the feathery antennae found on many moths, but these give the moths strong senses. The more feathery its antennae, the more surface area a moth has with which to pick up scent chemicals given off by other moths. A male silk moth's antennae can pick up the scent of a female from 7 miles (11 km) away.

Hawk moth

Bats and birds rely on moths for food. The elephant hawk moth has large eye markings on its body that help scare away such predators.

Tau emperor moth

Tau emperor moth

The rabbitlike "ears" of this moth are actually feathery antennae that help the moth find mates.

Bufonophobia and Ranidaphobia

FEAR of TOADS and FEAR of FROGS

Toads and frogs are closely related. The names for the phobias connected to them come from the most common species of each—*Bufo* and *Rana*. Fear of toads is more common than fear of frogs, but both animals have features that people find unpleasant. Amphibians, like toads and frogs, must stay wet at all times, so they secrete mucus, making them slimy. Toads have warts, too, which bufonophobes find distressing.

Creatures of mystery

Frogs and toads seem mysterious because during the day and when it is dry they hide under rocks, in the ground, or in the water. At night and when it rains they suddenly appear from dark places.

Wart warning

Perhaps because their skin is covered with wartlike knobs (sometimes these are glands for secreting poison), a common belief in folklore is that touching a toad can give you warts—not true!

Frog with markings—sufferers find the skin of frogs and toads off-putting.

Long jumper

Frogs can leap up to 10 times their own body length, which would be like a human jumping more than 50 feet (15 m).

Small green frog

Bright green frog

Poison pal

One reason to fear frogs and toads is because many species are poisonous. They use poison to protect themselves against predators, and frogs may also use it to protect their moist, sensitive skin from bacteria. One frog poison, called batrachotoxin, is among the most deadly poisons known—just a tiny amount can kill a human. Unfortunately for South American arrow frogs, their defense mechanism makes them very useful to local hunters, who get poison for their arrows and darts from the frogs' sweat, which they scrape off the backs of the animals.

Frogs all over

The bad news for ranidaphobes and bufonophobes is that frogs and toads can be found everywhere! They live on every continent except Antarctica. In the far north, there are species that can survive being frozen solid thanks to a sort of antifreeze in their bodies. In the deserts of Australia, the water-holding frog can survive some of the driest conditions on Earth by staying in a burrow for up to seven years, waiting for rain.

Cane toads can squirt poison from their shoulders.

Cane toad

53

Megalophobia

FEAR of LARGE THINGS

A humpback whale jumping right out of the ocean

African elephant

Charge!
You do not need to suffer from megalophobia to fear 16,500 pounds (7,500 kg) of elephant charging toward you!

Megalophobia is more than just a fear of large things. Megalophobes describe feeling that massive objects are looming over them, or that the gigantic size of an object or landscape upsets their normal ideas of scale. This leaves them feeling intimidated by their own size in comparison. Even just a picture of a large object, such as a cruise ship or an iceberg, can trigger a megalophobic reaction.

Giant redwood

Nature's giants

Giant structures and objects made by humans are the usual focus of megalophobia, but the natural world is also full of terrifying sights for those afraid of very large things. Humankind has contributed to the extinction of giant animals—or megafauna—in the world, such as the mammoth (a mammal related to the elephant) and the moa (a flightless bird). But the largest animal that has ever lived is still swimming in the ocean right now—the blue whale.

Loud and hungry

Even if you are not afraid of giants, the blue whale is huge. It can be up to 100 feet (30 m) long and weigh 200 tons (180 tonnes). A blue whale's tongue is as heavy as an elephant! Yet these giants eat only tiny shrimplike krill—up to 4 tons (3.6 tonnes) a day. They can live for 100 years, swim more than 20 miles per hour (32 km/h), and make noises so loud that they can be heard from a distance of 1,000 miles (1,600 km).

Big tree

Megalophobes beware—California's Redwood National Park is home to the tallest living thing, a giant redwood tree called a Hyperion. It is a massive 379 feet (116 m) high.

Autophobia

FEAR of BEING ALONE

Although it sounds like a fear of cars, autophobia actually comes from the Greek *auto*, meaning "self," and so autophobia (also known as monophobia) is both the fear of being alone and the fear of oneself. Probably the most autophobic animal should be Lonesome George, thought to be the last surviving Pinta Island tortoise. Lonesome George is native to Pinta Island, part of the Galápagos Islands, and has been looking for a mate for decades, but all the female Pinta Island tortoises are dead.

A herd of zebras

Running with the herd

If autophobes could choose which animal to be, they would have a wide range of extremely social animals to pick from. For instance, many species of large herbivorous (plant-eating) mammals gather in herds for protection against predators. Zebras live in small family groups, but these combine into herds of thousands.

Honeybees

Crowd of bees

Honeybees live in colonies (groups) or hives of around 50,000 individuals. In a colony of that size, a honeybee would find it hard to be an autophobe. Even more rare are autophobic ants and termites, because these creatures live in colonies of up to a million individuals. Probably the biggest group of animals in the world, however, is a school of Atlantic herring, which can include tens of millions of fish.

Reindeer on the move

Reindeer, also known as caribou, gather in herds of up to 500,000 animals. Every year, they travel a distance of up to 1,600 miles (2,600 km). An autophobe might prefer to be one of the trees in the taiga (northern forests) where many reindeer live. A tree in the Russian taiga, one of the world's largest forests, has billions of neighbors around it.

Reindeer gather together.

Ailurophobia
FEAR of CATS

From the ancient Greek *ailuros*, meaning "cat," ailurophobia is a fear of cats. Ailurophobes break out in a cold sweat when simply looking at a picture of a cat. If one approaches them, they develop rapid breathing (hyperventilation), an accelerated heartbeat (palpitations), and feelings of suffocation and panic. What is it about cats that can inspire such fear?

A longtime favorite

Cats and humans go back a long way. When people started farming, they would collect lots of grain at every harvest, but storing grain attracts mice and rats, so cats became useful as pest control. In ancient Egypt, cats were so popular that they were worshipped and mummified.

Witch's pets

Superstitious beliefs about cats seem to focus on black cats, perhaps because black is the color of night and death. Black cats are said to be unlucky, and the most common witch's pet is a black cat.

Avoiding eye contact with a cat simply attracts it.

A yawning house cat

Open wide
Yawning signals feeling relaxed, and yawning at a nervous cat can help to soothe it.

Siberian tiger

There are not many tigers left in the wild, because of hunting and the destruction of their habitats.

Run, but can't hide

Being hunted by a tiger would be enough to make an ailurophobe of anyone. Tigers can swim, run fast, and leap up to 15 feet (4.5 m) in the air. Adult male Siberian tigers can weigh up to 660 pounds (300 kg) and have been known to kill and eat adult bears! On the whole, however, tigers are shy and not aggressive, and only attack humans when they are desperate or too old and sick to catch normal prey.

Even playful kittens can terrify ailurophobes.

Tiger, tiger

If ailurophobes are frightened of ordinary domestic cats, they will be terrified out of their wits by their wild cousins, which include some of the most fearsome predators on land. The biggest of them all, the Siberian tiger, has massive canines and huge, muscular forelegs, which can kill a deer or a wolf with a single blow.

Kittens play fighting

Phobias of dirt and disorder

The fear of dirt and disorder is a major symptom of the sometimes serious mental illness known as obsessive-compulsive disorder (OCD). People can also have specific phobias relating to dirt, mess, and decay without having full OCD. In fact, humans have learned to dislike dirt because it can cause disease, but doctors also think that too little dirt can harm the immune system.

Ataxophobia

Ataxophobia is the fear of disorder and untidiness. *Ataxis* comes from the Greek word for "disorder." Humans generally like to keep their homes and workplaces neat and tidy, but animals are messier. Possibly the worst place for an ataxophobe to visit is the chimpanzee enclosure at a zoo—chimps are known for throwing their poo around!

Automysophobia

Automysophobia is the fear of being dirty. From the Greek words for "self" and "dirty," automysophobia is not simply the fear of dirt, but the fear of getting dirty. Automysophobes should avoid the hippopotamus. Hippos spend most of the day wallowing in muddy rivers or ponds.

Hippos love to wallow in mud.

Slime mold on a pine tree stump
This strange organism is created when millions of single-celled animals come together to form a slimy puddle—not good for a blennophobe.

Orange slime mold

The slimy Pacific hagfish

Blennophobia

From the Greek word *blennos*, meaning "mucus," blennophobia is a fear of slime. Slime is usually made up of long sticky molecules that absorb water to create something halfway between a solid and a liquid. It is a useful substance for many animals, such as snails, slugs, and fish, which use a coating of slime to protect their skin. Perhaps the slimiest fish in the sea is the hagfish. To protect itself, it produces slime from pores all over its body. Attackers can be suffocated by the gush of slime.

Seplophobia

Seplophobia is the fear of decaying matter. From the Greek word *sepsis*, meaning "decay," seplophobia seems understandable as rotting food can easily make us ill. However, several cultures around the world and throughout history have deliberately chosen to eat rotting food as a delicacy. Dishes the seplophobe should avoid include *surströmming*, a Swedish dish made from herring left in the sun, and Icelandic shark and skate, which are left to rot before eating.

Phobias of plants

For most of human history, much of the world was covered in vast forests, filled with giant trees and strange life-forms growing from the rotting leaves and trunks of the woodland floor. Perhaps phobias connected to the forest have their roots in this long period when trees ruled the world and our ancestors did not dare to venture too far away from what they knew.

Hylophobia

The word "hylophobia" comes from the Greek *hylos*, meaning "forest" or "wood," and is the fear of forests. Hylophobes are lucky to be living in the present day. Very little of Europe and the USA are now covered in forest, but 6,000 years ago it was a different story. Since then, around 80 percent of the world's forests have been cut down.

The trunk of a 2,000-year-old tree

Destroying angel mushroom

Dendrophobia

The Greek word *dendron* means "tree" or "branch," and this is where the word "dendrophobia" comes from, as it is the fear of trees. California is home to the Sequoia family, which includes the giant redwoods, the tallest trees on the planet (see page 55). The oldest living thing in the world is a bristlecone pine called Methuselah, which is an amazing 4,771 years old. It grows in the White Mountains, in California. Trees can be poisonous as well—the Caribbean manchineel tree can cause burns.

Mycophobia

Mycophobia is the fear of mushrooms and toadstools, which are types of fungus. The difference between a mushroom and a toadstool is that mushrooms are usually edible and toadstools are poisonous, but mycophobes are scared of both of them! Some species of toadstools can have strange mental effects and lead to visions and hallucinations. The death cap is probably the most poisonous mushroom.

Beware of poisonous mushrooms.

Fly agaric mushroom

Death cap mushroom
The death cap looks similar to some edible species, but is probably the most dangerous of all mushrooms.

Dangerous mushrooms
The destroying angel mushroom (left) is extremely poisonous, as is the fly agaric (right).

Death cap mushroom

63

Pain-related phobias

Specific phobia of pain is sometimes called odynephobia, but there are also many other types of phobia that relate to the fear of pain. You may wonder why we should have pain at all? Pain is useful—it alerts you to an injury or other problem, and it helps teach you to avoid harmful things. People who cannot feel physical pain are at risk of severe infections and injuries. Pain is also unpleasant, and disliking it is perfectly natural. Pain phobias, however, are extreme.

Amychophobia

This phobia is the fear of scratches or being scratched. Amychophobes have plenty to fear from animals—anything with claws, talons, or nails can scratch. Plants are just as bad. Possibly the scratchiest plants in the world are cacti of the Opuntia family—they have two types of spines and they are each as bad as the other. The big spines have vicious barbs, making them painful and difficult to remove, while the microscopic spines are small enough to float in the air and can get into your mouth and eyes, where they cause excruciating pain.

Cnidophobia

Unfortunately for cnidophobes, who fear stings, stings can be found across the animal world, from tiny creatures that cannot be seen without a microscope, to enormous ones like the lion's mane jellyfish, which can be up to 150 feet (46 m) long, including their long tentacles. Cnidophobes hate scorpions, which are related to spiders and carry venomous stingers on the end of their tails. Deadly scorpions can be identified by their straw color, long, slender tails, and thin pincers (claws). Stinging fish include stonefish, scorpion fish, and stingrays.

Phagophobia

The danger of being eaten should frighten anyone, but people who suffer from phagophobia (from the Greek *phago*, "to eat") are afraid that they will be devoured even when there is no risk. In the modern world, the chances of actually meeting an animal capable of killing and eating a human are slim.

stinger of a scorpion

Cnidophobes do not like scorpions.

Toxiphobia

Toxiphobes fear that even the most innocent food or drink might poison them. Some may even insist on preparing all their own food to make sure that it is safe. One food that a toxiphobe would never eat is fugu, or puffer fish. In Japan, it is a highly prized delicacy, but the puffer fish contains a deadly poison called tetrodotoxin. The poison is concentrated in certain parts of the fish, so it is possible to separate the tasty flesh from the toxin.

Burdock flower head with prickles

Blue-spotted stingray

Parsley seed burr

The stingray has a stinger on its tail.

Seed of destruction

This seed-containing parsley burr looks vicious to an amychophobe, but it causes no pain to an animal when it sticks to its fur.

65

Weather phobias

Life on Earth is only possible thanks to our planet's atmosphere, which keeps in heat and moisture and protects us from the deadly radiation of outer space. The trouble for weather phobes is that with the atmosphere comes the weather.

Cheimaphobia

Cheimaphobia, also known as cheimatophobia, is the fear of the cold, frost, and snow. The worst place on Earth for the cheimaphobe is probably Antarctica, an entire continent of constant snow and ice, where the average temperature on land is -58°F (-50°C). A body temperature of below 95°F (35°C) endangers human health and leads to death by hypothermia, so an unprotected person will not last long in Antarctica. With no chance for the snow to melt, all the frozen water that falls onto Antarctica becomes ice, forming an ice sheet that is nearly 1.5 miles (2.5 km) thick. This sheet contains masses of ice, which contain about 70 percent of the world's freshwater.

Snow at the top of a ski resort in Canada

Lilapsophobia

Related to astraphobia (see page 24), lilapsophobia is the fear of tornadoes and hurricanes. Tornadoes are violently rotating columns of air with the highest wind speeds on Earth—they move at speeds of up to 300 miles per hour (480 km/h). Tornadoes form wherever warm, wet tropical air meets cold, polar air, but by far the worst place in the world for lilapsophobes is Tornado Alley—an area that experiences more tornadoes than anywhere else—in the middle of America, including parts of Texas, Oklahoma, Kansas, and Nebraska.

Twisters can drop from the clouds without warning.

A tornado takes hold over Wyoming.

Hurricane storms

A tornado is a relatively small-scale weather phenomenon, easily avoided by the lilapsophobe, who can simply leave the area when a storm threatens. Hurricanes, however, are weather events on a much bigger scale. If you live near the coast in the Tropics, you may not be able to avoid being caught up in one of these monster storms, in which hurricane-force winds may cover an area of 500 miles (800 km) across.

Sense phobias

We rely on our senses to provide information about the world. Without them, we would be deaf and blind, and unable to feel or smell. But what happens when we start to fear what our senses are telling us, when we start perhaps to fear the senses themselves? Phobias connected to the senses are among the most disturbing and difficult phobias because they are so hard to avoid or ignore.

Ligyrophobia

Ligyrophobia is the fear of loud noises. Also known as phonophobia, ligyrophobia should not be confused with hyperacusis, which is an extreme sensitivity to loud noises caused by the ears' not working as they should. Ligyrophobes are advised to avoid animals like the howler monkey, which communicate over great distances by being extremely loud.

Haphephobia

Haphephobia is the fear of being touched. Also known as hapnophobia and thixophobia, this condition can be very isolating. Generally it refers to being touched by other people, but many haphephobes may also be entomophobes— afraid of insects (see page 42). Haphephobes may fear insects because of their multiple legs and long feelers.

Bush baby clinging to a branch—it has a loud cry.

Long antennae
The white-spotted sawyer beetle (above) has antennae that can be up to twice as long as its body. It uses its antennae to feel or sense its surroundings.

White-spotted sawyer beetle

The howler monkey's cry can travel 3 miles (5 km).

Skunk spray smells of burned rubber, garlic, and rotting eggs.

Geumaphobia
Geumaphobics have a taste-related phobia—a fear of new flavors, or of tasting something that they will not like.

Olfactophobia
Smells can trigger strong emotions and instinctive behavior, and this phobia is the fear of smells. One animal that takes advantage of this is the skunk. The skunk is a mammal famous for its defense mechanism— a smelly fluid sprayed from its backside. Strong muscles allow the skunk to hit a target up to 10 feet (3 m) away. The stench is so powerful that it can be smelled up to 1 mile (1.6 km) away!

Smelly skunk
The most common species of skunk has the Latin name *Mephitis mephitis*, which translates as "stench stench."

Striped skunk

Phobias of small things

Microphobia, a fear of small things, might sound odd—why should people feel threatened by tiny things? In fact, several more specific phobias, such as the fear of bacteria and viruses, fall under this heading, and they show that there is plenty to fear in the microscopic world, including the biggest killers on the planet.

Bacillophobia

The Latin word *bacillus* means "rod" and is used to describe a certain type of rod-shaped bacterium, but the word "bacillophobia" is used to describe the fear of germs in general. Everyone can catch colds caused by germs, and many people are affected by some form of more serious disease from them. Lurking around are scary organisms like the Ebola virus, which kills 60–80 percent of the people infected.

Bacteriophobia

Bacteriophobia is the fear of bacteria. The really bad news for bacteriophobes is that everyone has bacteria in their intestines. These bacteria help people digest food—it would be almost impossible to survive without them. Bacteria can also be hard to kill. Some species, known as extremophiles, survive and thrive in temperatures of more than 212°F (100°C), or in pools of acid that would dissolve human flesh.

Bacteria are dangerous, but usually too small to see.

Bacteria bloom in a petri dish.

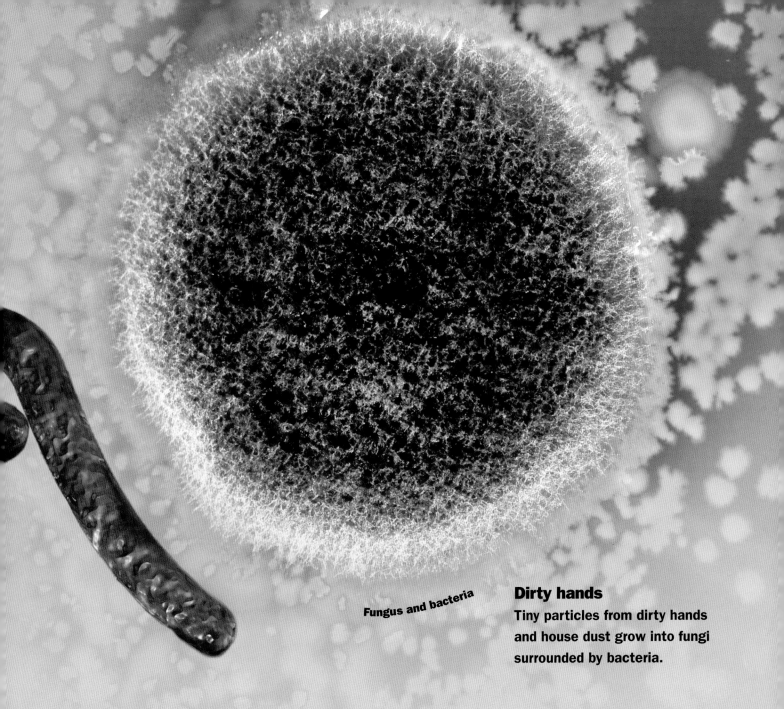

Fungus and bacteria

Dirty hands
Tiny particles from dirty hands and house dust grow into fungi surrounded by bacteria.

Isopterophobia

Unfortunately for isopterophobes, who fear termites, they are incredibly common. Related to cockroaches, termites are a pest species in many parts of the world, eating wood including floorboards, joints, and beams. The most advanced species of termites build huge mounds called termitaria.

Koniophobia

Few people give much thought to household dust, but koniophobes fear it. Perhaps because they know what it is made from. About 80 percent of the material you can see floating in a sunbeam is human skin shed by you and other family members. Other components of dust include house dust mites and their droppings,

fungal spores, insect fragments, carpet and textile fibers, hair, pollen, fingernail filings, ash, food crumbs, and even glass particles! Not a pleasant thought even if you are not a koniophobe.

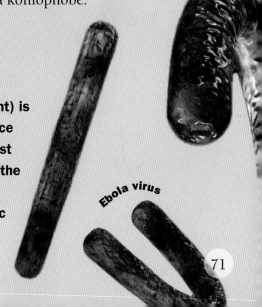

Ebola virus
The Ebola virus (right) is named after the place in Africa where it first appeared in 1976—the Ebola River in the Democratic Republic of Congo.

Ebola virus

71

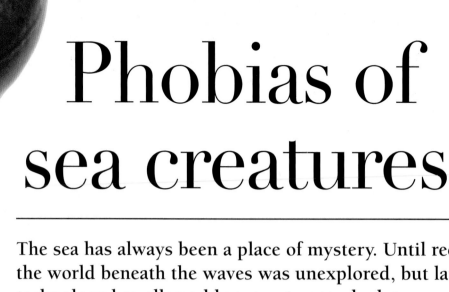

Phobias of sea creatures

The sea has always been a place of mystery. Until recently, the world beneath the waves was unexplored, but lately technology has allowed humans to spend a lot more time underwater. Even today, scientists know more about the surface of the moon than the ocean floor, which makes up most of our planet's surface.

A long, slimy eel

A giant otter feeds on its prey.

Lutraphobia

One of the more unusual phobias, lutraphobia, is a fear of the otter. There are many different species, but the lutraphobe's least favorite is probably the giant otter of South America, which is up to 6 feet (1.8 m) long, as big as a man.

Ostraconophobia

Many people are allergic to shellfish or have had a bad experience with food poisoning. Shellfish can easily pick up food-poisoning bacteria because of the way they feed. But ostraconophobia (from the Greek *ostracon*, meaning "shell") causes fear simply when the sufferer looks at shellfish, as they can often appear slimy and unappealing.

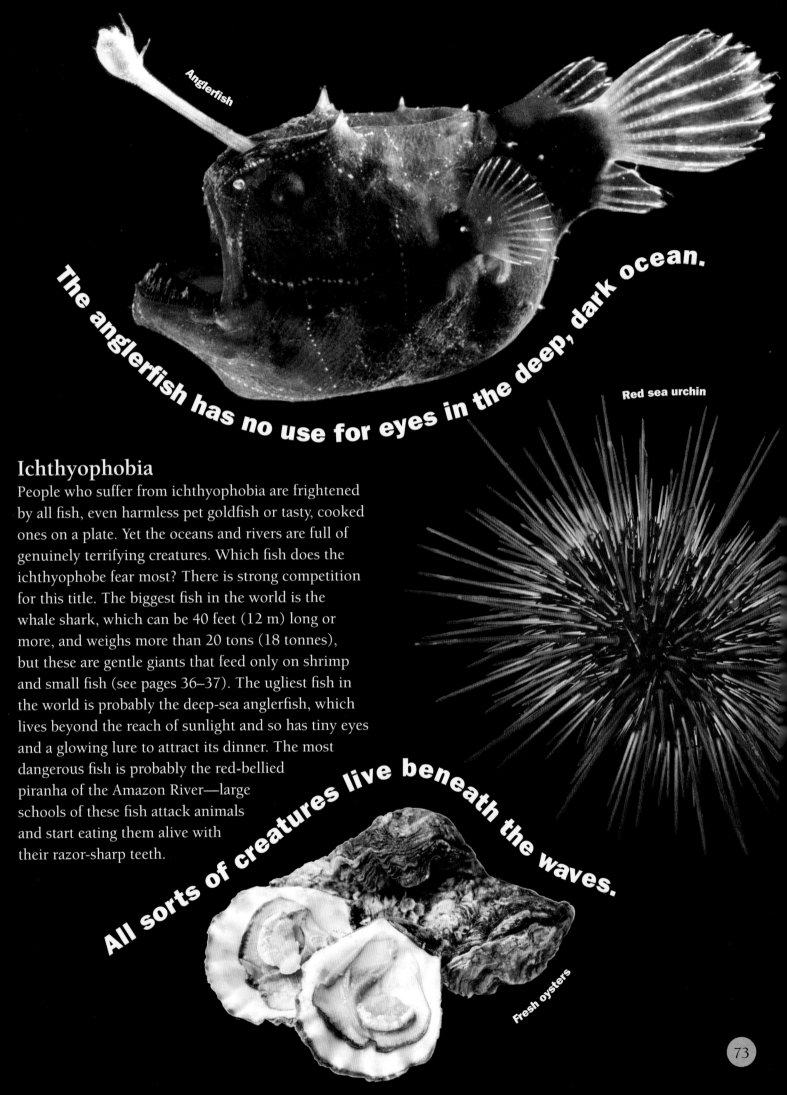

Anglerfish

The anglerfish has no use for eyes in the deep, dark ocean.

Red sea urchin

Ichthyophobia

People who suffer from ichthyophobia are frightened by all fish, even harmless pet goldfish or tasty, cooked ones on a plate. Yet the oceans and rivers are full of genuinely terrifying creatures. Which fish does the ichthyophobe fear most? There is strong competition for this title. The biggest fish in the world is the whale shark, which can be 40 feet (12 m) long or more, and weighs more than 20 tons (18 tonnes), but these are gentle giants that feed only on shrimp and small fish (see pages 36–37). The ugliest fish in the world is probably the deep-sea anglerfish, which lives beyond the reach of sunlight and so has tiny eyes and a glowing lure to attract its dinner. The most dangerous fish is probably the red-bellied piranha of the Amazon River—large schools of these fish attack animals and start eating them alive with their razor-sharp teeth.

All sorts of creatures live beneath the waves.

Fresh oysters

Color phobias

Color phobic people must be jealous of dogs and cats because they do not see color as well as humans. It is a myth that they can only see in black and white, but while humans have three color receptors in their eyes, dogs and cats only have two. Color phobes can avoid color by going out at night when the light is low and colors are less scary and bright.

Black leopard

Ereuthophobia

For humans, red—the color of blood—generally indicates danger, which may explain why some ereuthophobes developed their phobia of the color. The color red often signals that something is wrong or dangerous. It can have the same meaning in the animal world—for example, the bright red of a ladybug's shell warns birds that it is protected by foul-tasting chemicals. But in nature, it does not always mean danger. The color can also be due to a diet rich in red pigments, as seen in flamingos and ibises, which eat red crustaceans and plankton and turn pink or even bright red as a result.

Scarlet ibis

Melanophobia

Melanophobes are afraid of black, a color associated with night. In the natural world, the color black may help to disguise night predators. One of the best known black animals, the black panther, is really a different form of big cat—it is called a jaguar in the Americas and a leopard in Africa and Asia. Panthers have normal markings, but they are masked, or hidden, by dark skin and hair.

Xanthophobia

Yellow pigmentation is common in nature, which is not good news for the xanthophobe, who fears the color. Among insects and amphibians, it is often a warning signal to frighten off predators.

Amazon tree boa

Leukophobia

For leukophobes, white is not a good color! White can also spell death in the natural world—at least for albino animals. Albinos lack the ability to make skin pigments and so appear white. In the wild, this makes them stand out and so they do not usually survive for very long. Polar bears appear white for a different reason—their fur is made up of hollow hairs that reflect most of the light that falls on them.

Albinos may not survive in the wild.

Albino alligator

Glossary

amphibian
An animal that is cold-blooded, breathes air, needs to stay wet, and to live near water. Amphibians have a pre-adult stage when they breathe using gills, as a tadpole does, before growing lungs, as a frog does.

anaphylaxis
A type of very severe allergic reaction, caused by a substance or toxin, called an antigen, to which the body has become hypersensitive.

ancestor
A person who is related to another, who is from the past.

antidote
A medicine or substance that counteracts a poison.

antifreeze
A substance that lowers the temperature at which a liquid would normally freeze.

bacteria
Microscopic, single-celled creatures that spread easily between plants, animals, water, air, and soil. They bring about decay and can cause disease.

blood pressure
The pressure, created by the heart, that keeps your blood flowing around your body.

defense mechanism
The way in which an animal responds to danger.

diurnal
Describes a creature that is active during the day. It is the opposite of nocturnal.

edible
Suitable to eat.

feces
The remnants after food has been digested.

fungi
A kingdom of the natural world, which includes mushrooms and toadstools.

hallucination
A waking dream, in which you may experience something that is not really there.

hemisphere
Half of planet Earth. The northern and southern hemispheres are divided along the equator.

herbivore
An animal that eats plants.

hypothermia
A condition caused by being too cold, in which the body temperature drops dangerously low.

insomnia
The state of being unable to sleep over a period of time. Having insomnia can make you ill.

megafauna
Giant animals, both extinct and living— mammoths and elephants are megafauna.

metamorphosis
Transformation from one body form to another— for example, caterpillars become butterflies.

molecule
Two or more atoms joined together.

morbid
Related to death.

mythology
The study of myths and legends.

nocturnal
Describes a creature that is active at night.
Bats are nocturnal.

ovipositor
The egg-laying tube found in insects and fish.

palpitations
Quick, strong heartbeats.

paralysis
The state of being unable to move.

pigment
A color-producing chemical
that occurs naturally
in animals and plants.

pollination
The transfer of pollen to a
plant so that it can produce
seeds. The transfer is usually
carried out by insects.

prehistoric
Describes a time before recorded history.

rodent
A family of animals, including rats, mice,
and rabbits.

taiga
Northern forests of pine trees.

toxin
A poisonous substance.

tsunami
A giant wave caused by an earthquake,
landslide, or asteroid impact.

venom
Poison produced by an animal for attack
or defense.

vertigo
A feeling of dizziness and loss of balance,
often experienced when at a height.

Index

Acknowledgments

Marshall Editions would like to thank the following agencies for supplying images for inclusion in this book:

Key: t=top, c=center, b=bottom, l=left, r=right, bgr=background

Cover, clockwise from top: Shutterstock/Petr Jilek; Shutterstock/NatalieJean; Shutterstock/Alexander Raths; Shutterstock/Volkova; Science Photo Library/Tom McHugh; Shutterstock/Steven Maltby; Shutterstock/Connie Wade

Pages: 10l Shutterstock/Damien Herde; 10c Corbis/Reuters; 10r Shutterstock/James L. Davidson; 10–11 Shutterstock/James Steidi; 11tr Shutterstock/Cathy Keifer; 11b Shutterstock/ifong; 12 Shutterstock/Kevin Day; 13 Shutterstock/Vladimir Wrangel; 14–15 Corbis/Jose Fuste Raga; 14 Shutterstock/RM; 15 Corbis/Ferry Tan; 16 Corbis/Andrew Parkinson; 17 Shutterstock/Andrea Seemann; 18t Shutterstock/Eric Isselée; 18c Shutterstock/Maria Dryfhat; 18b Shutterstock/Helko Kiera; 19t Shutterstock/fivespots; 19c Shutterstock/Anatema; 19b Shutterstock/Anite Patterson Peppers; 20l Nature PL/Brandon Cole; 20r Shutterstock/BW Fasom; 21t Nature PL/Doug Perrine; 21b Photolibrary/Peter Weimann; 22 Nature PL/Jurgen Freund; 23 Nature PL/John Cancalosi; 24–25 Shutterstock; 26–27bgr Shutterstock/Korionov; 26 Shutterstock/orionmystery@flickr; 27 Shutterstock/Michael Lynch; 28bl Shutterstock/Art_man; 28–29 Shutterstock/Tatiana Makotra; 29br Shutterstock/Tramper; 30 Nature PL/Kim Taylor; 31l Photolibrary/Dennis Kunkle; 31r Shutterstock/Nito; 32tr Photolibrary/Barry Mansell; 32c Nature PL/Stephen Dalton; 32b Shutterstock/Vasilieff; 33tl Photolibrary/Malcolm Schoyl; 33br Photolibrary/James Hager; 34–35 Shutterstock/Val Lawless; 34 Shutterstock/J Klingebiel; 35 Shutterstock/Pavel Mitrofanov; 36–37 Shutterstock/Brandelet; 37tr Nature PL/Bruce Rasnar/Rotman; 38 Shutterstock/Doglikehorse; 39 Shutterstock/Mana Photo; 40l Shutterstock/Kletr; 40–41 Photolibrary/Gary Tack; 41t Shutterstock/Anobis; 41br Shutterstock/Kletr; 42c Shutterstock/Koshevnyk; 42b Shutterstock/Luis Louro; 43t Shutterstock/Eric Isselée; 43b Shutterstock/Image Focus; 44b Corbis/David A. Northcott; 44–45 Shutterstock/Cathy Keifer; 45 Shutterstock/Dr. Morley Read; 46 Shutterstock/Floris Slooff; 47t Shutterstock/Melinda Fawver; 47c Shutterstock/Eric Isselée; 47b Shutterstock/Emilia Stasiak; 48 Nature PL/Stephen Dalton; 49t Nature PL/Barry Mansell; 49b Nature PL/Visuals Unlimited; 50 Shutterstock/Cathy Keifer; 51tl Shutterstock/Pan Xunbin; 51tr Nature PL/Stephen Dalton; 51b Nature PL/Hans Christoph Kappel; 52 Shutterstock/Richard Peterson; 53tl Shutterstock/Jens61er; 53tr Shutterstock/Vladislav Susoy; 53b Shutterstock/Art_man; 54l Nature PL/Tony Heald; 54–55 Nature PL/David Fleetham; 55r Shutterstock/Urosr; 56l Shutterstock/Hedrus; 56–57 Nature PL/Staffan Widestrand; 57r Shutterstock/Andrea J Smith; 58b Shutterstock/Csaba Vanyi; 58–59 Shutterstock/Dennis Donohue; 59b Shutterstock/Lars Christensen; 60–61 Nature PL/Bruce Davidson; 61cl Corbis/Norbert Wu; 61tr Shutterstock/First Class Photos PTY LTD; 62l Shutterstock/Lauren Cameo; 62br Shutterstock/Style-photography.de; 63l Shutterstock/Wacpan; 63r Shutterstock/Martin Fowler; 64 Shutterstock/Matthew Cole; 65tr Shutterstock/Kiorio; 65bl Shutterstock/Roman & Olexandra; 65br Nature PL/Solvin Zankl; 66 Photolibrary/Kelly Funk; 67 Corbis/Jim Edds; 68 Shutterstock/Edwin Verin; 69tl Alamy/John T. Fowler; 69tr Ardea/Thomas Marvent; 69b Shutterstock/Eric Isselée; 70–71bgr Photolibrary/Laguna Design; 70bl Shutterstock/Alexander Raths; 71t Shutterstock/Brian Maudsley; 72t Shutterstock/Krasowit; 72b Shutterstock/Stephen Meese; 73t Nature PL/David Shale; 73bl Shutterstock/Dima Kalinin; 73br Shutterstock/Steven Maltby; 74l Shutterstock/Pan Xunbin; 74r Shutterstock/Eric Isselée; 75t Shutterstock/Five Spots; 75b Shutterstock/M.Kuperus